COME UP, HITHER

Thirty Days to Deeper Communion
with Yeshua Hamashiach

ANDREA MOSIER

BALBOA.
PRESS

A DIVISION OF HAY HOUSE

Balboa Press books may be ordered through booksellers or by contacting:

Balboa Press
A Division of Hay House
1663 Liberty Drive
Bloomington, IN 47403
www.balboapress.com
1 (877) 407-4847

Because of the dynamic nature of the Internet, any web addresses or links contained in this book may have changed since publication and may no longer be valid. The views expressed in this work are solely those of the author and do not necessarily reflect the views of the publisher, and the publisher hereby disclaims any responsibility for them.

The author of this book does not dispense medical advice or prescribe the use of any technique as a form of treatment for physical, emotional, or medical problems without the advice of a physician, either directly or indirectly. The intent of the author is only to offer information of a general nature to help you in your quest for emotional and spiritual well-being. In the event you use any of the information in this book for yourself, which is your constitutional right, the author and the publisher assume no responsibility for your actions.

Any people depicted in stock imagery provided by Getty Images are models, and such images are being used for illustrative purposes only. Certain stock imagery © Getty Images.

Print information available on the last page.

ISBN: 978-1-9822-2646-6 (sc)
ISBN: 978-1-9822-2647-3 (e)

Balboa Press rev. date: 04/22/2019

Contents

Day 1

Is the Day of Oneness

Beloved, come up here where I Am. It is the deepest desire of your heart. This is not covetousness. It is the desire to be like Me, to know Me, utterly. All that I Am is Provision for your daily life: the substance of a day is the substance of your faith, alive in Me. That is your Provision and it is enough. The ungodly seek the things that blind them from seeing Me. The ungodly seek moth-eaten garments, things that wear with use, things that thieves break in and steal away, the things that rust with age.

Beloved, come up here.

The future can change the past because I Am, always. I am being-ness.

Whatever happens in the future has already happened in the past. The evidence of things not yet seen. I see the evidence because I Am. I am Always-ness.

Today is the evidence you are seeing for tomorrow, but the substance, in ingredient form, already exists. It has existed from the foundation of the world. It has always existed. That is why you must be willing to obey.

Hear My Voice! I am always speaking. The lover of your soul does not sleep nor grow tired of you.

1

Come up here.

The perfect will of My Father is the exponential increase of the seeds of your life into a field of full manifestation where you and I will Live, Move, and have our Being-ness.

Unbecome what you no longer wish to be.

If you start thinking it's impossible it's because you have an imp on your shoulder telling you what's possible. You need to tell him where to get off.

Embrace a new language. Any other language will work. Try all of them. Speak in tongues, take a chance that your words will be washed and made alive. Speak Life Abundant. Let Life fall from your lips into manifestation in your Beingness. Believe you receive what you want when you pray.

Will your Heavenly Father give you a stone for the Bread of Life? If you ask for the Holy Spirit to fall on you, will your Heavenly Father give you a scorpion?

Perish that thought.

Cast down imaginations and every high thing that exalts itself against the Most High.

Come up here above the confusion.

I give My Mysteries to those who stay, get quiet, in being-ness, with peace. I give the keys to the kingdom to the left out, the lingerers, those who tarry, hungry for Me.

Those who rush wind up in traffic jams.

Come up here.

Day 2

A Day of Abundance

Every river has a mouth; the mouth of the river is the place where it spits itself out into the sea. With your speech you carry yourself into the next level, the next dimension.

The next adventure.

Sets your sights on a horizon.

I know my plans toward you, Beloved.

Rivers of Living Water are moving in your Spirit. Deep calleth unto Deep. Do you not know My Voice? I am the Voice of Many Waters.

It is still, small at first, and, like rivers rush toward gorges great with power to heave an endless supply over mountain ledges, my Voice moves mountains, carves canyons, makes a way in the wilderness, Beloved, but you must speak Me out.

If things are not working for you, maybe you're out on a ledge or off the main path in My permissive will, and now you're in uncharted territory, unfulfilled. Or maybe you see through a glass darkly, a shadow of the vision, but not the full light of what is before My Face.

Maybe you are listening to the wrong voice.

I had to put to death some things in you, carve off the dross, expose the light.

You may have been uncomfortable. This is not intended for your destruction.

I know the plans I have toward you, plans to bless and not to diminish. Plans to increase, not to destroy.

The blindness comes from what you perceive to be your past.

An illusion of the shining one who comes, shining with reflected light.

He has no light in himself, for he is a created being.

An illusionist.

He has nothing in Me.

The things you are holding onto are not only anchors, they're sepulchres. Dead men's bones. You hold onto what you fear to lose. That's called compromise. I didn't call you to that. I called you to joy, victory, overcoming resurrection life.

In Me, you move, live, and have your Being-ness.

God is Light, and in Him is no darkness at all.

Your invisibility has come only when you have mirrored other people, thinking it's really you.

Find your horizon. Lift up your eyes unto the hills from which cometh your help. Because only in this way can you keep Hope alive, and Hope is the loveliest of things because it springs from Me.

I Am your Hopefulness.

I know My plans for you.

To do My Will is not grievous.

Find your horizon.

Take out your map and plot your course.

Make your plans, follow your charts.

For I am the map, the course, the plans, the charts, the River, and the ship.

I Am, Always.

Day 3

Manna

Beloved, Healing is the children's Bread.

Rise up from your couch, from your bed!

Prepare to receive!

The seed is your Word, is in what you say, the Word in your mouth. It is near you. It is in your hand to do. Join with Me.

Manna-festation.

Mercies new every morning.

Begin Every morning with Me, Beloved. Let My mercies wash over you, cleanse you from the burnt ashes of the previous day.

Let Me give you Beauty for ashes. Let the previous day burn down and out like a spent cigarette. Toss the ashes and give Me your day.

Manna is fresh each morning; you will find that manna spoils if you keep yesterday's manna sitting around the house in ash-heaps like old cigarettes in ashtrays.

Let go of the things that have stolen from you.

There is no making it right.

It was never right to begin with.

And nothing of beauty was ever made with ashes.

Now, Faith is. Today. Give us This Day in Holy Matrimony to Me, the Lover of your soul. Is there any comparable?

What a difference a day makes. A day with the Lord is as a thousand years.

Do you now see what this means?

Give us this day, our daily Bread.

Why do you wait for me among the tombs, among the ash heaps, hanging out among the dead and buried? Why do you still wear burial clothes? Do you not know that I Am the Resurrection and the Life?

Lazarus, Come Forth!

I am not in the tomb. I am Life Abundant.

Come unto Me, all ye burdened down with the albatross of spent days. Cast off thy care. Give Me your burdens. It is My great pleasure to keep you in the paths of perfect peace! Come unto Me, My Beloved. Your great burden is not yours to bear. I need no martyrs or saints.

Take upon yourself My Righteousness. Walk out of your prison and into my Grace, sufficient for each day.

Cast your Bread upon the waters, for it will return to you after many days.

I Am that Bread of Life.

Your Provision. Your Abundance.

Let My Truth flow like a river out of your spirit and into your eternity. Let it be the Now Word for your life, nanosecond by nanosecond, moment by moment, until you build your spiritual life, your house, this tabernacle, from the abundance of My Word.

I am not only beyond time and space: My Word traverses and has traversed the planck distances. I have broken down the wall of separation between seed and plant, inhabiting the molecular structures of the unseen world, speaking Myself into the earth, born, living, dying, descending to Sheol, choosing to take your unworthiness upon

My Tabernacle, releasing the captives, resurrecting to Life Incarnate, ascending to the Father so that you could have Resurrection Life and have that Resurrection Life toward Abundant-ness.

Let your heart speak and not your mind still sifting the ashes of burnt down dream-houses. Those were not of my making. I am burning down houses of refuge where thieves still pillage the fragments of death and ministers of death still investigate the scene of the "crime." I have set fire, I have burned with the power of my lips the house of the old man.

Walk out of the remains of the day.

Exit the tomb.

The Spirit and the Bride say, "Come."

Come up hither.

Day 4

A Day of Hope

Beloved, do not despair. Grief is but a longing. I have put a longing in you to be with Me and bring others into our fold. That desire to bring the orphans without Me under your roof, to mother them, to father them, I have placed that longing within you: we are searching together to save that which is lost.

The pearl of great price in the parable: Was it not worth every sacrifice? To the merchant dealing in pearls, does he not know what he has the moment he sees it? In secret, He goes and offers Himself, all that He is, all that is His by inheritance, and places it at the feet of His Father for that pearl created in secret, made without hands.

Oh, this pearl is worth any price. Who sees the work performed in secret, the grains of sand breaking down the fleshy interior of the oyster shell? Is it not a miracle of transformation? And yet, all the while the breaking down of the flesh occurs, no human eyes can see the fruit of the sea born in that unlikely oven of time and a work done without hands.

I am the Lord Thy God, and I love surprising you with beauty. Your God surprises. A hawk circling on the coldest of January mornings. A cardinal on your front porch in a season when no cardinal should be that far north. Did you not sense it? A yard sale with every cookbook you ever wanted, dozens of them, all for ten dollars. A hand to help shoulder the load at the moment you are ready to leave it all on the side of the road. A friend calling you, "out of the blue," as they say, just when you're ready to give up on love, on your mission, just when you think all is lost. Someone you just met, willing to help you move.

Seek out precious pearls. Look for them everywhere. Seek and ye shall find. Have you found your pearl? Do you see them in the deceptively ordinary things in your house? In your neighborhood? What is the pearl of great price in your life? For what are you willing to trade mediocrity? For what will you risk all that you have to believe, for a moment, that there is more than tradition, more than working for bread that is not life, more than the dream-killing labor you do for others who hold the notes for your great debt. What are you paying for daily, monthly, yearly, that is no pearl in this life or any other? There is nothing of earthly value that equals the perfection of the pearl made without hands, without price.

But not without cost. You will have to give up some things. Pride in what you can do alone. The need to be right all the time. Your unfaithful eyes, searching always for an immediate savior that pacifies but never satisfies. Your life as an escape artist, running away from Me.

Bitterness over the unfair deal you got.

You are a pearl living within that fleshy house you call a heart. In that temple, that room, I am doing a work. I work out the sand and grit you think is your life and replace it with rarified symmetry, a gem never touched by the destroyer, nor by man's hand, but formed in time and grit and flesh by the Master's hand, brought forth like a child from a womb, complete, lacking nothing.

Pearls are not made to stay in the shell. They are made to bring forth, to display in a string of pearls banded together with others, to create pearlescence. To open the eyes of the blind to beauty's true work. I give beauty for ashes, pearls for grit. Open your heart to the work of My Hands. A city set on a hill cannot be hid. Butterflies from cocoons, magnificent blooms from a thistle, even dandelions whisper this message.

The lilies of the field wear their fine-spun garments, the kings of the plain, visible for miles.

To the blind eye, all is darkness, and this is the nature of what the world calls "depression," a spiritual blindness: the inability to see the color of hope. But I have cocooned you in hope, a thing that lives. Hope is the puppy bouncing through the dog-door, entering the house, jumping up into a waiting lap, unable to contain itself. Hope bubbles up through the springs of your soul, breaking the dry ground like laughter. Hope is the loveliest of all things because it is the door to all the others. Without Hope, there is no vision, no way of seeing the Grace I have already given, no room for Faith to operate, to plant itself, to bring forth its fruit: Love, Joy, and Peace.

Don't discount Hope. Hope is the greatest conduit of all good things. It is first through the door of your heart. It is the first stirring of the soft part of your heart, like the first pristine flakes of a great snowfall, cleansing the landscape, a place in the tender parts of the flesh where the grit and sands of time make an imprint. Hope is a Place, a place where faith will combine the elements to bring forth the pearl I gave everything to possess.

Day 5

A Day of Peace

Your day begins with a cup of coffee, or, perhaps, sustenance in a bowl, or a sandwich wrapped by strange hands delivered in thin paper through a window. It is in this space and time the worry begins.

Before you know it, you are thrust into your day, premeditating the work, the load, the weight of a day balanced in the scales. A day you have not quite entered yet. The white paper of this day pushed across a desk, your mission handed to you. You have not read its contents, and already you are in deep waters. Your anxiety weighs you down, the chains you wear pulling you under the surface of troubled waters.

And yet, your spirit is dry. How can you drown in such dry territory? And yet, it is the angst of your every day.

Beloved, do you not comprehend the environment I have created within you? The Kingdom of God is inside you. You were not meant to live in parched, dry land. Deep calleth unto deep. Communion is there. Come to the River. Love is there. Hope is there. Grace is there. Joy is there. Faith is there. The boldness to face a day, to stare it down until it slinks off, every worry sliding off to nothingness like the ashes of a fire rise on the wind and blow into distant places to be remembered no more.

Since you were recreated, transformed into My likeness, your natural habitat is water. By nature, you cannot drown. Please remember this! Out of your innermost being flow rivers of living water. This water liberates, sets free, breaks chains, opens prison doors, shatters walls, windows, and strongholds. Annihilates guilt. Pulls down imaginations and every high man-made fortress of worry, obsession, and fear. But you must speak to your day, write on the page of your day. You must cast down the imagined day you have created for yourself out of this mighty fortress of worry and strife. If you do not, the page will fill just as you have imagined it. With your mouth, with the force of your will, you create chaos if there is chaos in your spirit.

I did not create you to inhabit dry places devoid of my Being.

It needs to rain in your house.

Let it rain. Let My Word bring rivers of living water to the dry, parched, useless land in your spirit. Let the Word break up the soil, renew the ground. Let the seedlets grow into a garden filled with fruit, for I come to consume the fruit of My vineyard. See that I do not find a parched, dry land, for I have invested so much in You. Everything that I Am, I have given so that you might enjoy abundant life.

I cannot inhabit dry places. The Holy Spirit cannot live in deserts with only thorns, brambles, and unstoppable winds blowing through miles of barren landscape.

You are My garden. I have come to abide with you.

Have Me for coffee. When you rise in the morning, cast the care away and talk to Me. Pray in the Spirit, and allow My Rivers of Living Water to enter your being, flow out of your life, and manifest abundance everywhere. My Water is free, but this lifetime lived in this dimension, this dispensation, is short. Avail yourself of the Living Spring now. Look at me, look into My Face, memorize my countenance, not the landscape of an imagined day.

A day will come when the springs in the earth will dry up. The earth dwellers will then know how much your very presence among them brought them Grace by association. Favor, granted by close proximity. Because you were there, I was there.

You cannot get water for another. Beloved, I have designed your water to rise, overflow, and wash over others. That is your purpose, to bring your anointing in the presence of others. I send my rain upon the just and the unjust.

Make it rain.

That is your true purpose.

Anything less is a barren wasteland.

Day 6

A Day of Awakening

Your spiritual eyes must be opened. Have you been asleep? Arise, My Beloved, set sail. No man can stop you. Open your spiritual eyes to the possibilities. Have you fallen out of love with the familiar? It is no wonder. Blindness loves nothing more than to lead the blind. Did I not tell you? The love of many will wax cold, and they will fall out of love with what they worship because it does not illuminate. Those with no light seek others to proselytize. This is the height of their insecurity, to heap to themselves followers: this to validate their own lost way.

Blindness is an inability to see the truth; most of all, you will be blinded to the truth about yourself, about how you are in the world.

If your right eye offend thee, cast it out!

What has distorted your vision? To the pure, all things are pure.

Idolatry is a giant: something looming so large in your vision that you see nothing else. The "beam in the eye" in the Gospels. This beam blinds you to the way you are in the world. All you can see is the speck in your neighbor's eye.

Offense is always a product of idolatry.

What is your god?

I Am the Way, the Truth, and the Life. I Am the Light of the world. A city set on a hill cannot be hid. I bring the Light of My Essence -- you -- out from Myself into the darkness, set you high on a mountaintop.

I build the temple. This building's framer is God. I Am the Chief Cornerstone.

Come, Beloved, come now to your Refuge, to the Rock that is higher. This building fitly framed together groweth unto an holy temple in the Lord: In whom ye also are builded together for an habitation of God through the Spirit.

You are My House. Do not languish in confusion. You are not going to the House of the Lord. You are the House.

This is the Unity I told you about in John 17. I have reconciled all things to Myself.

Look through My eyes, and you will experience a revolution in "seeing." What is familiar will fall away, dead to you, the deadness of false security you have gathered around yourself. This familiar scent of death will no longer comfort you. You will no longer find its fragrance desirable. Your very spiritual senses will grow keener than those of the flesh, and you will sense the heavenly fragrance of life, of My Being, the Rose of Sharon, the spikenard and the cypress vine, the fragrant wine of our communion.

Our garden mingles, the flowers blooming where waters run freely in the plains of Hebron. In your spirit, the Living Waters give birth to Beauty Incarnate, the very fruit of Love Himself. I Am that Body of Love. I Am that Living Water. The birth of Love in your spirit thrives in this garden.

Seek My Holy Reservoir. Seek the Baptism by My Hand, endless Water from on High, from the High Places. Let this water cleanse your innermost being. Let the water cleanse your spiritual eyes and let the dead world fall away from you like scales. Watch the old familiar transform into a strange, new world of possibilities. Watch the dead things to which you have clung with desperation melt and morph into nothingness.

Embrace your new way of seeing. See the worlds I have framed with My Word, the beauty of a transformed moment. See my Love inhabiting all creation, the manifestation of My Being tabernacling among you. For I have chosen you to be My Habitation. This is my chief desire: to give you life and to abide with you, My Beloved.

You are the Light of the World. A city set on a hill cannot be hid. Bees gather around the hive. The birds have nests. There are houses of honor, but My House, saith the Lord, is a Holy Habitation unto My Glory.

You are my Workmanship, My Poems, built up to harbor only Me. Your life is a poem written by Me, did you not know this?

How long will you waste your time writing the rehearsed lines of a fleeting moment of time, a fragment of space that even now is passing into nothingness? How long will you write the same page of time past over and over again?

Right now, I am calling you to live the poem I have created inside your spirit. You know when you are not living poetically according to My perfect will. I am this Poem, and yet, each is distinct, as you are distinctly Me but in such varied manifestation as expresses Me fully.

You cannot do it alone.

I give people for thy life.

Command ye me concerning the works of My hands. I am doing this work in you.

Seek Me early and seek me late.

Tell Me what you desire. Let me have your dreams.

Commune with Me. I, alone, know you.

No dream can match the poetry I have invested in you.

I gave all for it.

Day 7

A Day of Gathering

A daily thrumming of a world in business like a great engine steams along its course. Negotiations, sales meetings, people talking across false walls in office buildings.

Cubicles. It's a small world, and a cold one, in the world of business.

If you take up the mission I've offered you, there is something you must know.

You are not in business to be busy. You are not in business to make mammon, neither are you to serve mammon.

You are on a gathering.

It is a harvest. You are fishers of men. You must take people to coffee, to breakfast, to the park to walk and talk.

Gathering people was my specialty during My earthly ministry. I gathered them at seaside, preached to them from a boat, taught them at temple, spoke to them in their living rooms, at my house where there was no more room and still they came.

Once they let someone on a bed through My roof.

When the word gets out, some will gather. Those with ears to hear. My sheep know my voice. They know to gather when storms are near. They hear me when I speak to them, and they come.

The mission of gathering is easy. It is best done one at a time. Put bait on a line. I will tell you what to do. You will know. Nothing contrived. It's best to allow Me to shepherd the flock. Those who come are those who hear Me and want to know Me.

Let it be your kitchen table, or the parking lot at the shopping center.

You don't need a fancy building. You aren't working by yourself. I have other laborers. If My people answer the call to gather, we will bring the harvest in. Those you reach can reach others in ways you couldn't. That's how it works.

It isn't hard. My yoke is easy, the burden light.

Think about it. Gathering is a natural thing. If you open your eyes, you will see how it is done. We gather daisies, coffee spoons, eggs, buttons, roses, paperwork, marbles, silverware. We gather the remnants of a day, the last vestiges of a bygone era, the last rays of a summer sun late in the evening, on those longest days when the gathering night seems far away.

In that Day, saith the Lord, they will have no need of a teacher, for I will teach them My Ways. Every man, woman, and child will learn of Me. I will pour out My Spirit upon the sons and daughters, upon young men and old. People will report having visions of Me, dreaming dreams of themselves ministering in the power of My Spirit.

The might of men has never saved a single person.

There has never been a time such as you are living in. Humble, ordinary men, women, and children working in fields are breaking up the ground of clay hearts and bringing in my harvest. You are My hands, My feet. Be swift and ready to move out at a moment's notice. Eat the ready bread of Passover. Take life in your hands and take Me as your Provision. Break bread with the hungry. Bring the New Wine to the table, and let My sheep drink.

This is My Body. Broken.

My Body, those called by My name, are leaving the churches lulled to sleep by skilled salesmen preaching the gospel of mammon. But, behold My Body, coming out of Egypt now, eating the bread of readiness, feet shod with the preparation of the Gospel. How beautiful, to watch them walking out, an exodus, like watching fireflies drifting out to sea. They are leaving the shadow of death.

Bring them to the Table I have prepared. Take ye, eat. Taste and see that the Lord is good. The Lord is thy Shepherd.

I Am that Passover Lamb. Bring them to My Table. Let them learn of Me.

For I Am meek and lowly of heart.

And My table is full.

Day 8

A Day of Agreement

You are moving into a day of Perfection, meaning, Maturity. You are growing up! I Am that Perfection. I bring you to maturity, like the bud on the vine turns, spirals, into the perfection of the rose. In arcing toward perfection, you are coming into agreement with Me. I Am the Author of that perfect will for your life. Of course, you are living in an imperfect place, but come up here with Me! Here, in the place of refuge, in the quiet space of your heart, in the broken-up soil of that place, I will plant Myself, in Living Word form, and you will hear My perfection spoken in your spirit. I Am that Word spoken in secret, and I Am the manifestation of that dream, formed in what you call "reality."

I Am the quiet word. When you are washing the dishes, I Am the Lover of your soul moving up behind you, speaking lovely things in your ear. I speak in the quiet natural light of day in the shop. I Am the quiet voice speaking to you before sunrise, calling you to enter fellowship. I Am in longing to join you for coffee. Would you make time for Me? I promise, I will make it worth more than you could ask or think.

The world rushes by, chasing dimly-lit dreams, working for inconsolable lusts, the need for validation through heaping up of store.

They have their reward. Oh, I have blessing such that there is not room to contain it, but of my stores there is no end. The oil and the meal never run out. No thieves touch My Provision. But material goods last but a season. You know this. Shiny and tempting, these base goods lose their brightness, their allure. But the shoes of the Israelite children never wore out. My manna, like My mercy, is new every morning. My Gift is perfect, wanting nothing. The Lover of your soul knows you. The world does not. Companies chime in on the airwaves, offering you all manner of things you never wanted.

I have come that you might have Life and have it more abundantly.

But you must get into agreement with Me. In My Word, you have read that when two or more are gathered together there I Am in the midst. And as concerning anything, if two or more pray in My name, I will grant their request.

Let your conversation be in agreement with My Word. Put yourself on the pathway to the complete fulfillment of the dreams I placed in your heart before your birth.

We are two. Let it begin here.

There are mission orders for you. But as long as My People continue building shrines to their own lusts, I cannot grant their requests. There is a thief at work. Here in the earth, moths eat; rust corrupts.

But if you gather to yourself the souls in darkness, if you bring them into the Light I provide, I will give you a blessed life, a vibrant abundance, awakening desires even you forgot you once had, long ago, when you believed in the brightness of My Return.

When you believed My Word and simply performed My Word.

Walk in the Light as I Am in the Light.

When I look through the darkness, let it be the Light of the World burning up the murky depths of this present darkness. Let candles burn;

let your light so shine before men. I have made them thirsty, desperate for Me, desperate for the Light.

I cannot go without you.

Pierce the darkness. Leave the comfort of your so-called "sanctuary," and go into the fields where others carry the light. Open your eyes, your heart, to opportunity. Do not ask if I have chosen you.

Go ye into all the world.

Day 9

A Narrow Path

I was not sent by My Father to make bad men good.

Are you still trying to become good?

The Cross is foolishness to those who are dying. That's because the world believes the way of the world is right. To men, the way of other men seems right. How many different bandwagons, programs, company philosophies, buzz words, political campaigns have come and gone, birthed and now dead, out of the world's sense of the "righteous cause."

Seasonal, at best.

The world's wisdom is foolishness to Me.

They keep expecting Me to behave, to think, to act, as they do.

The dead cannot comprehend the living.

Here is truth: All bondage is born out of bondage to self. If you are your own god, you have a hard taskmaster, and anyone who loves you has an even harsher master.

Notice how no one can measure up to your standards.

Beware, however, the measuring rod you use to evaluate others; that same measure will be used to judge you. When was the last time someone measured up to your expectations? When was the last time you measured up to your own?

Your Heavenly Father does not expect perfection apart from My redeeming Love. You must be born of Love: the rebirth. But you must die to the god of self, the harsh master exacting perfection and never getting it. Every sickness, every trauma of your life, is born of the circumstantial law you created and upon which is based every exchange you have with all the individuals you know and love.

Conditional love, which is never born of Me.

You love those who love you. You love those who are like you. You love those who give you what you want.

A love I did not place in your heart. For by that measure, you are lost, for you cannot ever measure up to My Measure. You cannot calculate My Worth. You cannot fathom the Unfathomable. My Height, My Breadth, My Length, My Width, the dimensions I pre-exist, the walls of existence I shatter with My Omnipresence, you cannot comprehend. No intelligence can. Will the clay say to the Potter that forms it, "Why do you make me thus?"

The god of self tries to slip into the wedding party wearing moth-eaten garments, mere filthy rags. Because the world is his mirror. He is fashionable, she is in vogue, she thinks, because she wears what everyone else is wearing. He wears the suit of acceptability.

That is religion defined. A gathering to congratulate each other on their fashionably acceptable lives.

That god must die. The god of self is already dead. That is what you must know.

The Father welcomed the Prodigal Son. He did not wait until the Prodigal Son became "good." For what is "good" to you? What would the world do with true goodness?

I'll tell you. The world would do what My People did over 2000 years ago. Unredeemed man, the dead, will put to death that which is Life because they comprehend it not.

Let Me remove the blinders so you can tell the dead from the living.

Rise up from your deathbed and learn of Me. Let Me bring you the Living Water that revives, brings to Life.

I look not for goodness. I look for those who recognize the deadness of this present darkness, the deadness of religion, the putrid stench of the world's lusts that never fulfill and never have.

I look for signs of life, for those who have yoked together with Me, who follow Me on a path that is far less traveled. A narrow way. Only those who hear My voice will enter this pathway and walk it, for it is not the broad nor popular street. Not everyone walks this path. This path is foolishness to the dying. Dying people have a lot of company on the broadway to destruction. This expansive road is well-lit with false light and seems right because it is a popular road. Many have found it. The god of self approves. It is destructive because its light is deception, its promise fleeting, its end temporal, the finish line, destruction.

But you are running a race. The path is hidden to those who are perishing. I Am your Shepherd, and I Am your Victory. I stand even now, at the finish line, having run your race for you. It is not by might, not by power, but by My Spirit, saith the Lord. I run when you are weary. You shall walk and not faint. I will raise you up. I run when you sleep. Your spirit and mine traverse the planck distances, the dimensions unseen. The road is hidden from the destroyers, the lustful, heaping up for themselves rusting treasure even now losing its sheen.

But you are not running for filthy lucre. I Am the Way. My Word is a lamp unto thy feet, a light unto thy path. I named the stars; shall I not bring you into glory to the wedding chamber, to feast with Me? Shall we not drink wine and break bread together?

On this narrow way, I Am your Sustenance. I Am the Pathway under your feet. I have ordained your steps, like hinds' feet, pressing your tiny foot into My footprint. It is our signature. Your tiny footprint in Mine. That is the victory. I have overcome the world. Walk ye here, in these steps ordained from the foundation of the world.

Come up into the high places, step for step, and follow Me. I will show you great and mighty things ordained from the foundation of the world. The secrets of the universe spoken in your ear, in your dreams.

You have only to lose the bondsman that requires too little and takes too much. He who loses his life will find it. Your life is hid in Me! Let that bondsman be crucified with Me. Let the god of your self-righteousness die daily. Take up your cross.

And follow.

That is your true work.

Day 10

A New Day

I Am in the business of newness of life, and it is the season. It matters not what age or time of life or how many new starts you have asked for. This time, the new thing is of Me, it is My doing. Let the weak say "I am strong." Let those who walk run without weariness. The fresh rains have begun. Let the young and old gather in the fields, in the streets, in the parking lots and coffee shops, teaching and learning and sharing My heart.

I Am the God of New Foundations, of new bends in the road. The wind has shifted. A refreshing has begun. You have labored under the yoke of unbelievers, shouldering loads these taskmasters have no intention of lifting. They have not helped, no one has stopped to lift the load, but I am calling you to cast all your care, the weight of every burden, over on Me, and receive your rest.

Come unto me, all ye that are heavy laden, burdened down with the weight of men and women seeking self-satisfaction, those who fail to comprehend your worth. Yoke together with Me, and we will do a New Thing in a New Season. Let the winds of change blow through your house, your room, there where we abide together.

I watch you, waiting for you to stop trying to "fix" your life.

Lay it down.

Come into fellowship with Me. Bring Me into every aspect of your life. Stop parceling your life into divisible pieces. Is it any wonder you feel so fragmented?

Do you not know you are meant for Me alone?

We are creating a garden of communion.

Let the winds of change bring the fragrance of our garden in your workplace, on the road to work. Rekindle friendships. Reach out to the brokenhearted, those in need, those bound with chains of addiction, with anxious thoughts. Seek those in bondage to the flesh.

Enter into that rest, the rest that transforms. The sabbath begins now. Rest your mind on Me. Rest, knowing I have overcome the world. The victory is already yours. The power of My resurrection lives in your spirit, changing landscapes, bringing rains to the dry land, transforming deserts into lush gardens.

The natural man cannot inherit the things of God. All the flesh wants is dead on the vine before it satisfies. Wormwood. The flesh trades the eternal for the temporal. It has always been so. The flesh turns gardens into deserts.

Come into our garden where it is always Spring. Our garden yields grapes, choice fruits, trees of healing fruit. Let the winds of resurrection refresh your spirit until your flesh is put to its only fit work, baptized in the washing of the water of the word. Let your mind be renewed, by that baptism, the latter rain bringing these favorable winds.

Beloved, be ye transformed. See yourself in the garden of our communion, the warm wind kissing the faces of the flowers clothed in finery, the same wind that bathes our faces. Walk among the cypress vines, in the olive groves. Move into celebration. Move into festival mode. Let there be robes, and rings, and the fatted calf brought to the table.

Do not fear these winds of change. We are the springs of living water, respite to a dry land.

Drink ye the new wine, so much better than old wine. Dance in the rain drops and watch the droplets dance on puddles, eddying into riverlets teaming with possibilities. Never before in the history of the world have there been so many possibilities, so many moments of a day open to the Good News. Because never before have there been so many hungry for My Spirit. Yes, there is need, but the rain is here! And it is Springtime, time for dancing, for celebrating Newness of Life. Break out the banners! Spread the tables! Sound the trumpet! Call in the hungry, the thirsty, and tell them there is sustenance without price. The season has come for the Newness of Life.

Day 11

The List

Have you ever tried to prioritize your day? A day seems an insurmountable obstacle set in front of you. You look at the monument to progress before you: stacks of bills, requests from well-meaning people, the needs of family, the list of obligations.

You are making a list. Whether you realize it or not, you are sending a message each day, each hour. Every second of living a cloud of witnesses watches your decisions. What you have done, what you will do, what you are doing and thinking right now: all these coexist in a place you are creating.

What you do is either fleeting and already dead or it is eternal and catapulting you into a life abundant. These micro-decisions weigh exponentially into your days because they make other decisions you have not considered.

You tell people their importance in your life by your actions, or, more to the point, inaction. In this passive state courtesy of technology, people live virtually but not actually. You are only self-actualized to the extent that you advocate for your life in the Spirit and for others' lives in the Spirit.

You tell your spouse you love him or her. But you are making a list. You tell that person every minute where they fall on that list. In the same way, and more heartbreakingly, you tell your children where they rank on your priority list. Does every person on social media come before the people in your house? If not, why not set the phone down? Count up the hours you spend. Facebook does. Instagram does. Every app keeps account. Do you, Beloved?

Where do I fall on the list? Do you rise with thoughts of Me to begin your day? You come home, exhausted. You want to unwind. Full of anxious thoughts, you seek to avoid Me. And, by association, you seek to avoid the people who love you. Some of My people show their children indifference, paralysis, indecision, and neglect. It crescendos until they find themselves alone. Their children tune them out.

I Am not a God of Lists. I Am Lord of Fellowship.

Beloved, come up hither.

Your real life is hid in Christ. It is not plain what you shall be on the day that you see Me face-to-face. Are you ready for that face-time? Most people tell Me they are not. They confide in me that they hope I will wait and maybe not return today. Their list is long. Their lives are temporal. They have "so many things to do." I wish I could say those things were life-changing, world-shaping things. I wish I could say that the list of "things they have left to do" included quiet time in deep fellowship with Me. Epiphanies, transformational truths I could whisper in their ears. Oh, if they could see that I am the only mirror that Transforms! Be ye transformed, Beloved, and never, ever try to conform yourself to the world.

What does your mirror look like? Whose approval do you seek? Are you still trying to "fix" yourself?

Let the dead bury the dead.

I have no fellowship with Belial.

I have come so that you might enter into that Rest. I promised you Rest, but so many of My people won't receive from Me.

You have medicated yourself with every possible remedy. Sleep aids, social media, endless strings of relationships that don't work. Your life has become predictable. You are running from a life you can't understand into the arms of disappointment, dishonor, and destruction.

Those things are not of Me.

Come up hither. Let us speak together of daily manna, eternity in the moment.

Here is a secret. What you do in your life, what you include in your daily list that is Eternal, never dies. It always exists, past, present, and future. The cloud of witnesses on high waits for you to take hold of this secret. You are creating your life. You. I have made it possible. This new man, this new woman, under the power of the resurrection, is creating a life. What do you want in your life? What would you trade for one thing you could count on, one Eternal thing? One True thing?

The Law of the Spirit of Life in Me has made you free from the law of sin and death.

Weeping may come for a night; but Joy cometh in the morning.

Come up hither.

Day 12

A Day of Feasting

Why do you wait for that which isn't coming, for that which fails to fulfill? Beloved, learn to celebrate My Goodness. I Am Chief Organizer of Festivals. Do you labor for a future day when all will be perfect and you can celebrate? Do you not understand that I commanded feasting? I Am the Lord of the Passover. I ordained the Feast of Tabernacles. I Am First Fruits. Celebration is part of the fabric of My people's daily lives. Each festival requires preparation. Special music. Special food. Tables spread. Everyone welcome. Mandatory presence. Banners of color and clean linen. Don't be missed! Come to the table!

And all this in the wilderness! Are you in the wilderness? Wandering in confusion, wondering where the path went? I prepare a table before you in the presence of your enemies. Is it time for feasting? Is it possible your rhetorical questions launched in My direction won't bring deliverance? What would darkness do if you set candles, fine plates, white linen, and stores of food provided by My Hand?

What if you bid those in desperate thirst to come to the table?

What if you came, Beloved?

What would happen if you chose to walk in paths beside the still waters? What would happen if you left the crowds in stores and traffic jams to find the green, grassy meadow and a soft place to fall? Might you enter into the rest I have provided?

Come to the table. Your presence is mandatory if you wish to receive. Feasting is now. It is ordained. Come to the table and receive plenty from My hand. Bless My Name. Recount the many good things that have come from My hand. Thank Me for those good things yet to come. Thank me for the loveliness of My presence in the world. For defeating the darkness and lighting the world with the smallest of fires burning in the spirits of those who have received Me.

Hold festival celebration in the light of those lamps of like-minded. Share the provision I Am, the goodness I Am, the Bread and the Wine spread among the multitude. I promise I Am more than enough.

For My tabernacle was among men from the beginning, and it was not necessary to wait until a permanent structure, a proper temple, could be built. I inhabit the praises of My people. And by the Holy Spirit, I have tabernacled among men in the temple made without hands. But there is no need to wait. This table is for wilderness wanderings and for entering into the promised land. This table is spread to the very edge with My goodness so that your enemies will see. Eat the ready bread and be ready to move the table. The Bread of Readiness moves with you. Hold festivals of celebration on your journey. Feed those you meet on the way. Spread the table wherever you may be along the path.

Why do you wait for events, happenings, perfection? Your destination is not an arrival. It is not an event. I Am the Way. Am I not perfect? Take your Provision with you and look for those whom I have called to come into the kingdom. Take up your mission. Live in Festival mode. Celebrate My victory. Does it matter what men do to you or say about you? Fear not men who can kill the flesh only. Reverence Me, the Author and Finisher of your Faith, the Holy One of Israel, the Lion of the Tribe of Judah. For all authority has been given unto Me over the power of the devil. I have risen, even I have defeated Sheol. I have taken the keys to hell and death. Therefore, you go out. Spread the table with healing, with provision, with daily manna so those I have called may know Me. Celebrate My goodness before you see any evidence of that for which you seek.

Do not bring unbelief to the table, nor fear. Do not bring murmuring, backbiting, complaining, ingratitude, criticism, anger, wrath, jealousy, slander, or idolatry to the table. This is a fellowship. I have no fellowship with darkness.

Walk in the light, even as I Am in the Light.

My ready bread is for those whose feet are shod with the preparation of the Gospel. It is the Good News unto salvation toward you who believe. You will know the murmurers if they are offended by your celebration of Me. If you lift My Name high and they are offended, shake off the dust. They are not welcome at the Table.

Throw off your mourning clothes. Cease to wear the sackcloth and ashes. For, I call you to a wedding supper. You will wear the white raiment I provide. Put on the garment I give. Throw out the red sash, the banner high and lifted up, to show your acceptance of My sacrifice, for I have given Myself for My church. Be the ready bride. Make ready for Me. For, behold, I return swiftly to take what is Mine.

Until That Wedding Supper, take the Cup of Betrothal, the Bread of Communion, and keep Me ever before your mind. Remember Me and I will write your meditation of Me in the Book of Remembrance. Fill that book with endless lines recording our fellowship together. Remember Me as your Friend, the Lover of your Soul, your Bridegroom.

Take the cup signifying our eternal commitment. Cleave to Me. Abandon all else that would take your attention. Give up fruitless pursuits. Find quiet time and call Me to mind, and I will enter your thoughts. This is the end of worry and anxious thinking. The Cycle of death-thoughts cannot coexist with meditation of Me. When you take Me into your thoughts, fear dies. Be mindful and conscious of Me always, as I am mindful and conscious of you always. We are destined to sit at table together in a place far from where you are.

But not far from where I Am.

It is at hand.

Come up hither.

Day 13

A Day of Surrender

Beloved, your true strength is surrender.

Do you have the strength to surrender? It is your abiding work.

Surrender to the will of the Most-High. How long will you compromise, settle, withstand, barter, plead for permission to enter into something that is not My perfect will? Do you think, somehow that you know better?

Is there any evidence in your life that this is true?

How many times have you sold out? How many times were you certain you were choosing Life, only to find the package wasn't what you really wanted? Be careful what you ask for, the world says; you just might get it. That is a truth. But if you ask of Me bread, will I give you a stone? If you ask for My Holy Spirit to baptize you with power from on High, will I give you a scorpion? Nonsense. Let it never be said.

My gifts do not bring sorrow. I do not repent of giving you good things. My gifts have no sting. I have taken the stinger out of that scorpion, Death. Where is its power now? What hold does it have on you? I'll tell you. The answer is: Death has no power over you forevermore. You have applied the Lamb's Blood to the doorposts of your existence, your habitation. You and your house are spared.

Resurrection is power born of surrender. Do you not see it? The seed dies to break out of darkness, something new, alive, wielding the creative power of light-energy. A force, no, not of nature, but of Resurrection Power! The baby surrenders to its birth, leaving its darkened chamber to break forth, a miracle of perfection. Every surrender to a death brings resurrection, transformation.

All true surrender is death.

Oh, Death, where is thy sting? Resurrection Life breaks forth, the surrender to lay down this body of corruption brings forth the body raised incorruptible. The restitution of all things will manifest before your eyes because of resurrection power, the power to make all things new.

The sower sows the word, and by that Word all things visible were made by a process that does not appear. Word-manifestation. The seed surrenders to the soil. The soil surrenders to the rain. The rain surrenders to the sun. The plant surrenders to the blessed environment I created in which you thrive. All things move toward the Face of God, who sends His rain to fall on the just and the unjust. The earth surrenders to His grace sprinkled all over the corruption. Grace, in the form of Love, covers a multitude of sins. Grace says, "Wait a little longer. Surrender to patience. Let patience have her perfect work."

Love is surrender of your will to My will. That will, surrendered, brings transformational love, resurrected marriages, revived parent-child relationships. For I did not come to do My will but the will of the Father Who sent Me. I asked the Father in Gethsemane if there was any other way, Beloved, do you not know this? Nevertheless, I said, not My will but Thine be done. I surrendered to the cross and became the first-born of many brethren.

Surrender always brings exponential growth.

A good yield.

Surrender builds bridges, creates ecosystems. It is the surest way to world-building.

Except a corn of wheat die and abide in the ground, it cannot bring forth fruit.

All resurrections begin with surrender.

Where in your life are the severed heads of garden flowers, the fallen soldiers of failed love, monuments to ambition that brought not only pain and pressure but also complete and utter loss? What relationship cost you something you weren't prepared to pay? Do you not know the meaning of redemption is counting the cost and paying it anyway? The pearl merchant gave all for the pearl of great price. He sold everything. He redeemed it for the price of His earthly life.

Paid in full.

It is finished.

Surrender your will to Mine. Do not be amazed at My vision for you. I placed it within you. My people claim they do not know what I want them to do, but deep down, they already knew this. Their destinies pull them like a homing pigeon is pulled back to the place it began, like a falcon returns to sit on the arm of his trainer.

My people simply don't believe I would dream a dream so large, so grand, for them to fulfill.

I did not "catch" you to trap you in a life you don't want.

Don't you have that now? A life you don't want? A story that didn't go the way you envisioned it.

Is it possible you misunderstood your role, thinking you were the writer rather than the pen?

Lay down your earthly life.

Our story is filled with adventure, brimming over with laughter, with love not yet put into words, with tender moments of truth in an intimacy you have only begun to comprehend.

I "caught" you to release you into the joy of My perfect will.

Surrender your stubborn will, your back-up plan, your second choices, your fall-back position, to My perfection. You are the pen of a ready-writer. Your life is written, and yet, you must allow the Author and Finisher of your faith to finish what He has begun in you.

The Transformation, evidenced in our story, together.

Surrender to the Story of Our Lives.

Day 14

Consummation: A Day in the Ark of this Tabernacle

You are told in My Word to "redeem the time because the days are evil." Do you know what this means? You are told in the Gospels that a day's evil is sufficient for that day. Do you understand this?

You have begun to seek Me early, rising with your thoughts turned toward me. You have questions. How do you surrender your will? How do you know My will for your life? How do you listen and hear?

The answer is contained in the mystery of the Church. This triangular relationship mirrors the relationship of the trinity. Earthly alliances can only rehearse and role-play for the sake of instruction the communion enjoyed by the Father, the Son, and the Holy Spirit.

We are a Family, and We exist in total communion with One Another.

The model I created for this is the marriage relationship.

This teaching on marriage was never meant to be taken literally. We understand that life is more than the literal walking out, in the flesh, every command in My Word. If we believe that every command is a fleshly command, we could, for example, read the scripture in Joel

2:1, Blow the trumpet in Zion, and, having been commanded thus, we would sell everything, quit the job, and fly to Israel to stand around and blow a trumpet. These things in the Old Testament are written for your edification, some things as a warning, others as archetypes for learning of the kingdom, others as prophecy.

The mystery of marriage is the mirror image it serves up of mutual surrender.

The marriage roles, then, are idiomatic and not to be taken literally. There is much mystery, and it pleased Me to create the tabernacle of marriage as the ark of My covenant, the light of the world. All families mirror My Holy Family. That is My perfect will. The eye cannot say to the hand, "I have no need of thee." A true marriage in total communion means that no member thinks of himself more highly than he ought but surrenders his will for the good of the marriage union, the family. Many of My people are unequally yoked with pagans, idol worshippers, who worship themselves and live to fulfill their own lusts. My people perish for lack of knowledge. You were not called to fulfill the lusts of the flesh, neither yours nor someone else's.

I have called you out of Egypt.

And yet, you are My Bride. Your surrender to Me is paramount. I Am a Husband without equal.

The woman's body holds the mystery of surrender. She is a precious vessel of Hope and Faith, a type of My Church, the Bride of the Lord. The man's body holds the mystery of true strength, that strength which surrenders to that Hope and Faith born within her. He submits his will to utterly save his bride, to create communion, just as I surrendered My will to the Father for the sake of the communion and perfect union of My family. And for the Restitution of all things.

I did this for the love of My Bride, the wildflower in the wilderness. My strength is made perfect in weakness as the man's body is saved through surrender bodily to the hidden chambers of a woman's heart. It is this surrender to her humility that mirrors the very act of salvation, and this continual surrender leads to the ultimate communion. Again, the earthly type is just that: a type. Nevertheless, people join themselves in merely physical union every day, in marriage, outside of marriage, never understanding this intimate act is but a rehearsal, a kind of role-playing, leading to a revelation of a greater understanding of the nature of intimacy between the Bridegroom and His bride.

He is provision; she is enterprise. She produces; he labors. She is the precious harbor of all things good; he must daily take up his mission to give himself for her, *being Love Incarnate and bringing all Goodness to her.*

I speak not of physical bonds of marriage but of My Church and of Me. The intimacy we share is the fruit of the communion I enjoy with My Father. And since the Holy Spirit is the Comforter, the Counselor, the Intercessor, and the means by which the rebirth occurs, the Holy Spirit, as a brooding, caring Person of the Trilogy, is like a Mother. And this is why My Church is the Gentile Bride and why Israel, the True Israel, is the Wife of YHVH. Through the power of the Holy Spirit is the Restitution of all things both in heaven and things on earth. Not by might, not by power but by My Spirit, saith the Lord.

Boaz is the husband. He toils in the wheat field, ordering His workers to bring in the harvest. It is the season, but the season of My rains will not last forever. Ruth is My Bride. She submits to Boaz's will, lying at his feet. When she chooses Him over all others, calling Him her preferred, the Chief among Ten Thousand, the Altogether Lovely, He presents the redemption fee to purchase back for her and her mother the land stolen from them. He takes her to wife, giving all that he is for her provision, for her life. They conceive and bear sons to take the fruit of their love into the generations.

The little crocus blossom of Kedar, the gentile bride of Song of Songs, living outside the covenant, chooses her Shepherd lover, preferring Him above all others. Betrothed to her, He goes away to prepare for her a place in Glory.

Such is the blessing of marriage.

A marriage with Me is to be fruitful, built on surrender, on honor and selfless giving of all for the other members of the family. It is an ark to harbor souls in safety and peace so the blessing may overflow to others outside the grace I have provided. There is no place for pride in marriage. A marriage partner does not exist to serve you, Beloved, to feed your lusts, to make you happy. Neither do you exist to fulfill these functions for your earthly marriage partner. You exist to serve Me and, in the marriage bond, to surrender to My will inside that ark. You are to produce fruit, maintain the blessing and grace of the Lord, finding grace in My eyes so My Glory doesn't depart from your midst.

Tame the tongue, for many little fires kindle and catch, burning up what you have built, burning what is laid up in store, stealing that communion in the ark of your safety.

Pull together to steer your ship in the same direction. Do not be unequally yoked with people who do not know Me and do not seek to do My will. When steering the great ship, both of you must steer clear of icebergs.

Do not interfere with what I Am doing in the midst of your partner's life. Let Me perfect patience and let patience have her perfect work. I Am capable of bringing My people to maturity. But you cannot make one hair on your head white or black. Why would you attempt to change your marriage partner to suit your will?

Not your will but Mine be done. That's what you must pray. Stand still and see the glory of the Lord do a mighty work. Let it be My work, not your labor, for no flesh should glory. Marriage is not a fleshly institution.

The marriage is a tabernacle only, a place of My habitation in the earth. When the earth passes away, when My people pass from their earthly lives, they will no longer have need of this earthly marriage ark. The tabernacle is for the wilderness. I have prepared a habitation for you. This habitation is rehearsed but never fulfilled utterly on the earth and won't be until I receive you unto Myself at the ingathering, the end of the harvest age. You will come into the wedding chambers and into the Marriage Supper of the Lamb, where you will be presented as My Bride. There will be no need of earthly marriage for My faithful Bride will be presented to Me that day, and so shall we ever live together in total communion with one another. This is the true communion, the consummation devoutly to be wished.

Let My transforming power bring you into full surrender to this mystery, to Me.

I Am your true Husband.

Behold, the Bridegroom cometh.

Behold, the Bridegroom already came.

He came unto His own, but His own received Him not.

I came as a Shepherd, and to as many as received Me gave I eternal life.

Pray earnestly for My swift return. Long for Me, as I long for you.

The bride in Song of Songs says, "Make haste, my beloved, and be thou like to a roe or to a young hart upon the mountains of spices."

Yearn, earnestly, for that consummation.

Day 15

The Day of Mountain-Dissolving

You have heard the phrase "mountains to the seas," and you have heard My command to say to *this* mountain, "Be thou removed and be cast into the sea." Oceans hide mountains, did you know this? The tallest mountain peak, taller than Everest, is under water. On the calmest of nights, ships' captains must navigate with care around mountains made of ice. The tip of the iceberg is but a small portion of that which is under sea level.

Have you ever thought about the reason for this command to speak to the mountain and cast it into the sea? Have you tried to climb every mountain, only to fall back and take territory you thought you'd already won? Are you weary with the effort of multiple attempts to reach the top, only to meet with the same result? Falling back to where you began?

What if I told you that mountain was not there for you to climb?

Surely, you say, you sent that mountain to me so that I could learn. Search My Word. Did I ever command you to climb a mountain?

What if I told you that you had created the mountain in front of you? Obstacles, obstructions. Strongholds, fortresses, towers. Man-made structures to put walls between us, between you and your enemy. And yet, you still can't see that you are your own worst enemy. You think a wall will stop the hurt, but how high must the fortress be to protect you from your own flesh? From me? Material goods, fine clothing, jewelry, cars, corporate ladders, all shrines to the flesh, so many walls to keep out the truth.

And so, before you know it, an insurmountable problem arises. Oh, you see the tip of the iceberg, but I've watched it form for so long. Hidden beneath the surface are the strongholds of fear and worry and strife, of self-doubt, and unworthiness, and addiction. And what can you do about it? You are not surprised.

And yet, your mountain is before you. What will you do? Show everyone how strong you are? Climb to bring attention to your endurance? Make excuses? What is your mountain? Depression? Cancer? Divorce? Hate? Unforgiveness? Hurt? Bitterness? Indifference? Unemployment? A passionless existence? Fear? Self-loathing?

Name your mountain. Use your authority. It doesn't matter how long the mountain has been there. Speak to it. It has taken up enough space in your life. Tell it, *Be thou removed and be cast into the sea.* Say to your mountain that it is under My authority that you say such things. Believe in your heart that I Am Enough. Grace covers a multitude of sins, and I have oceans enough to cover your mountain. The Voice of Many Waters has made it so.

The mountain will be removed from your path. You will no longer find yourself stopped on your journey. Your task was never to climb that mountain. Vaporize all obstacles. Pull down imaginations. Overthrow strongholds and every high thing that exalts itself against the name of the Living God. Come out with your slingshot and tell Goliath your plans for him. Run toward your problem. Tell your mountain, "This day has the Lord delivered you into My hand. This day will I sever your head from your body and feed your body to the fowls of the air and the beasts of the field."

The Lord is your strong tower, your fortress, and He is your refuge on High. Come up and enjoy His protection as He hides you in the cleft of the Rock. Let Him take you to that place of Safety, Beloved, but do not climb mountains of the world's making. You are not going where the world is going. You do not strive to reach ambitious mountain-peaks as they do. Your life is hid in Me. Let religion work people over; you are called to walk on the water, above the troubled waters hiding cavernous places and mountain ranges unseen.

Let the mountains and obstacles of your life go.

They have been there long enough.

Day 16

A Day of Substitution

In the Eighteenth Century, wealthy men would send their slaves into military conflict in their stead. The wealthy would avoid danger, deprivation, and death in wars these men often helped start.

True Humility came as a slave, willing to go into the war to end all wars over human flesh: a war waged in three days in the belly of the earth, where I took upon my flesh your sins until I was made sin.

Propitiation. Substitution. The offering of the Lamb on the altar of sacrifice. The soldier-slave who went in your place. The guiltless prisoner who died in a murderer's place, among thieves, crucified by robbers.

But it pleased the Lord to bruise Me, because heaped upon My flesh were the burdens of human sin, not only for those who believe, but for the sins of the world, if they would but receive this rare and precious gift. This gift, after all, is the Pearl of Great Price. For what other earthly gem is carved into perfection and redeemed from destruction by a Kosher Merchant who has no earthly business in goodly pearls. And pearls are earthly business created in mystery, shrouded by the toughened exterior, a chamber of safety: a womb.

I told My people, there shall be no sign given to this generation except for the sign of the prophet Jonah. Three days and three nights in the belly of the whale and coughed up onto dry land to prophesy of rain. *Repent*, Jonah begs of Ninevah, and Ninevah repents. What is repentance but a turning away from what is destroying you?

As My Father had to hide His face from Me when I took upon My flesh that which destroys the human race.

Three days and three nights I spent in Sheol, in the belly of the earth, suffering the penalty, complete isolation from My Father. I suffered in My flesh the wounds of men but that was nothing compared to the forsaking, the utter darkness without hope of reconciliation, separated from the Father for the first time in My Life.

I wept there, not for Myself, but for the countless earth dwellers who would one day know this pain, this futility, the endless darkness, the complete absence of love. For to take upon Myself your sin, I had to separate Myself from Love Incarnate, endure your penalty, so that mankind might be saved from this end.

When I watch you suffering the guilt of shortcomings, the anguish of loneliness, the frustration of a day, I wonder if you know how My Grace holds the world as you know it in place. I wonder if you realize the darkness that would encroach upon this planet, upon your very existence, if the Light of the World were suddenly taken out. Would you possess a sudden, stark realization of the many ways My lampstands lit your way, lighted the path beneath your feet, gave your days and nights a hope and expectancy of tomorrow? I have told you that each day possesses evil sufficient for that day. My mercies are new every morning. My rain falls on the just and the unjust. My manna falls from heaven, the revelation for a day more than enough to push back the enemies of Love.

You are not living through endless days of darkness. You, Beloved, are walking in the light, even as I Am in the Light. In Me is Life, and that Life is the Light of Men. I Am the Way. The Truth you seek was made flesh. In the belly of the earth, I heard My Father proclaim of Me, "Thy throne, Elohim, is Forever." We are one, a plurality, the Holy Trinity. It pleased Us to make man in Our image.

You are the Light of the World. A city set on a hill cannot be hid. I did not make you a candle among men only to watch you as you hide yourself in a dark corner. You were made to light up a room. The life of the party, you are, the host of the feast, the owner of the field. You are not a suffering servant. No man has sent you into the war in his stead. I am the First-Born of many brethren. You have come into the adoption of sons, into Holy Communion with the fellow-begotten in Me.

It has pleased My Father to do this, for His great joy is to have you cry, *Abba, Father*. We have this Union here, while you are in this tabernacle, sojourning through the earth, awaiting earnestly the transfiguration. For ye know not what Glory is to be revealed in You. For I have given you a transformational rebirth, the end of which has yet to be seen.

Your frustrations with yourself are not unlike the "growing pains" of teenagers whose bodies are changing exponentially. These changes, these groanings and sufferings in the flesh, are necessary, but you must appropriate my work on the cross and crucify your flesh daily. Your flesh is at enmity against Me, but I Am doing a work of complete renewal in newness of life.

Your path is lit. Your Way is unobstructed. Your chains are broken. The most precious gift from that pearl of revelation, when the veil is lifted, when all feast their eyes on Love Incarnate in the beauty and symmetry of Holiness, is the Freedom to be what you were all along, even when you were nothing but a piece of wounded flesh. It pleased the Lord to bruise Me, to make Me that wounded flesh, and now, out of that earthy substance in an unseen chamber, comes the total metamorphosis: that Pearl of Great Price in you. For I say unto you that these sufferings in your flesh are not to be compared to the glory that shall be revealed in you, the unveiling of that symmetry I desire.

This is the process of renewal. The daily loss of wounded flesh and the gaining of ground in the mysterious, hidden place, in chambers made without hands, the transformation, yes, the transfiguration, of daily living into symmetry.

What does it matter how long it takes? This is the entire point of living. To allow Me to create True Beauty in Love. To surrender the Pearl to My Hands.

What "work," Beloved, compares to this? What ambition exalts itself above My Work in you? Do you not know that all creation groans for this transformation? The earth, like a woman, travails, the birth pangs coming closer together as she hastens the day of this birth. The earth shall wax old like a garment, but by My Hands, Manna will one day manifest for all to see. The New Jerusalem will come down like a Bride adorned for her Husband, and My Kingdom will come upon earth.

Life will swallow Death in Victory.

There will be no need of the sun, for the Lamb Himself will be the Light.

There will be no more night, nor fear of what comes in the night, no more hidden terrors, and no more sea.

In those days, they will have no need of a teacher, for all My People shall be taught of Me. You, Beloved, will enjoy My presence in chambers not made with human hands. We will drink from the cup together in the fellowship of brothers and sisters, luminescent in white radiance, like strings of pearls, a thing of beauty earnestly desired.

Come, Beloved, into fellowship with Me, now, while Grace brings all things together in cohesion, holding back the onslaught of evil and darkness waiting to be unleashed upon the world. You are not appointed unto wrath.

Come, My People, enter thou into thy chambers, and hide thyself away with Me for a little while, until the indignation is past.

Come up hither.

Day 17

A Day of Unburdening

Blessed are ye when men persecute you and despitefully use you, for so persecuted they the prophets before you. Are you called to prophesy? Let it be known that jealousies arise based on the spiritual gifts. I give these severally as I will, but those who lust after the accumulation of goods believe in the world system, which says that for one person to achieve, another must be brought low.

In the Kingdom of God, it is not so. Did I not tell you this? Unless you come as a little child, you cannot enter. Babies do not know jealousies. They are not on the take.

Sweet words often bring bitterness. Love turns to pain. John, the Beloved disciple, said wormwood goes down sweet but in the belly is bitter. My Word divides the truth from the sweet lies of the god of this world. An illusionist, much of what he offers is sweet for a moment but bitter in the end.

The children of Israel grew jealous of Moses. They did not want a mediator between them and YHVH. They were unhappy with their daily portion and lusted after animal flesh. The sweet quail meat brought death while they consumed it.

There is one Mediator between man and YHVH. It is I. You are sojourning in a bitter country. I bring Manna with no bitterness, daily provision for your life. Look for My provision. Do not seek for that which the ungodly pursue with all their strength. They have their reward. Seek first the Kingdom of God. Come as a little child. Cast all your care upon Me.

You have heard this before. Still you do not know what it means.

Perhaps you still do not understand why I had to travel to the belly of the earth.

I have told you of this, of how your sin was heaped upon Me, along with the sins of others. All of mankind's sins were heaped upon Me. I became sin. I was made sin. I had no form or comeliness that any would desire Me. Those who saw Me in Prophecy, esteemed Me stricken, smitten of God. For this, I came into the world, that the world might be saved. Such is My Love.

But many do not receive My gift. They would rather chase down their sensual desires, fulfilling every one until, in the midst of consumption, just when the taste is sweet, they are consumed.

The wages of sin is death.

But I have come that they might have Life and have it more abundantly.

You are sojourning in a bitter land. It is not a hospitable place. There is an illusionist at work, but I have put him under My feet. I have triumphed over the forces of Sheol, I have taken back the keys of Sheol and of Death.

Now, hear Me again on this matter. Cast all your care upon Me.

Picture Me there, for those days in Sheol. Sin incarnate.

I came as the Lamb to give Myself in Provision for you.

Therefore, when I say, "Cast your care upon Me, for I careth for you," I Am able.

I Am saying, put all the bitterness, the angst, the anger, the lies, the slights, the grief, the neglect, the abuse, the unfairness, the violation upon Me. Tell Me you want a divorce. Tell Me of your wounds. Give them to Me. I was wounded for your transgressions. I was bruised for your iniquities. By My stripes, ye were healed.

Cast all the darkness, the confusion, the worry, stress, and strife on Me.

For I already carried it.

I already defeated it.

I give beauty for ashes.

Let me have the ashes of your day. The fragrance of your dawn awaits.

Day 18

A Day of Transformation

A new heart I will give unto you

A new spirit will I put within you

I will take away the stony heart and give you a heart of flesh.

A living organism is the oyster in his shell. The heart of flesh feels the pearl grown by accretion. This is his tiny burden, My yoke, the fruit-bearing, a small weight and not grievous. This production in secret, the daily work, My work, keeps this hidden flesh, this vulnerable flesh, in motion for the purpose of a miracle fruit.

Every river has a mouth. The oyster has a mouth, and flesh, and a beating heart. The oyster's mouth is a door to the soul. Every double-mouthed dagger, the double-edged sword of My Word, divides and distributes the breath of the Spirit, divining flesh from marrow, judging all deliberation, all thought life, discerning the shiny illusions of this present darkness and the moral intentions of the heart.

We hold every thought captive, a hostage to Truth, bringing down imaginations with this double-edged sword. Do you picture it? In My Word, I am revealed as the Lion of the Tribe of Judah, the Revealed Heir, Worthy to to take the scroll outlining the Will of My Inheritance, and to take back the land occupied by the usurper.

I Am the Landlord. My Word is the Title-Deed.

You are My joint-heir. I Am the First-Born of many brethren. You have been raised up together to sit in heavenly places with Me. You are already seated. Your name is on a card at a table of my choosing. I Am waiting for you, you are waiting for that inheritance, it has already been given, you are already here with Me, you are already seated.

Every tongue that rises against you, you shall put to shame. You are not created for shame, not in this life, and certainly not in the Kingdom of God.

You are My lampstands. I walk among you, a Priest Forever after the order of Melchisadek. Our Light illuminates the world. They have no idea. They have always had the light. They rely on it, but they do not comprehend the Source. For they say, "Where is the promise of His coming? Do not all things continue as they have from the beginning?"

They know not what they speak. For My Life is the Light of men, but they worship darkness. They glorify the works of darkness and comprehend not the Light.

You are My lampstands, lighting the Way to Me. My Word is the Lamp unto your path. Do not allow men to bring you to shame. Walk away if you must. Take My authority, Take My name, and stop the mouths of the wicked. Discern those among you who create chaos, catastrophe, working works of darkness in secret and manifesting a toxic environment, rivers of sewage, poisoning the lives of others.

I Am Life in you, so that you might have love, joy, peace, a life of abundance, the fruit of the Spirit manifest like pearls on a necklace, garlands and victor's crowns, for your race is already won, if you rest in Me. You have already run it. You wear your crown already. You cast crowns at My feet. You are already seated.

I have overcome the world. Why are you surprised that the world does not understand My Truth? Why are you shocked that the world comprehends not My Love? The world is dying. This you must know. The cross is offence to the perishing. This is how you will know them, by their continual offended state. In their self-righteousness, they react to their perceived slights, their so-called injustices. They are the center of their existences, never missing a chance to be the martyr but recoiling at the idea of My sacrifice. My People are not offended. They live in peace, in love, joyous in My Victory. I defeated Death. Where is its sting? I Am the Lamb slain from the foundation of the world. I have no equal, no adversary.

The stench and bitter pain of Death is at work in the chaos of the lives of those who are still lost in darkness. They heap to themselves people to share in that misery. In sharp contrast, My People, who are called by My Name, humble themselves and pray, walk in My Joy, embracing the work I performed in the Cross, applying My victory to their lives. They allow My Word to work in their spirits, transforming them into overcomers. This is the only fight: the fight to allow My transforming Work within your spirit.

But you must trade that heart of stone for a heart of flesh. In your vulnerability, My strength is made perfect. Those who hunger and thirst after Righteousness will be filled. The truly hungry will see the miracle of the loaves and fishes.

I Am not the God of the self-satisfied. I Am the God of those whose thirst has reached epic proportions, whose approach at the Well becomes an eternal baptism of Living Water, the Water I give freely and without price. That Water I have is yours.

But you must understand your own lack, your own thirst. Nothing else satisfies.

All other sources are, at best, temporary.

Is your well dry? Have you gone as far as you can on your own power?

Is your heart stony? Dry with the harsh and bitter wind of worldly cares?

Have you come to the end of yourself?

I have endless Rivers. Have you ever waded into the middle of a river on a hot, summer day? Have you ever played and danced and found complete joy in the midst of a river, letting the cold water refresh you, wading out in the deepest part and letting the cold water overcome you for a moment, then breaking the surface, refreshed?

Your destiny is Transformation. All has led to this moment. This baptism. Total immersion. Dive in. The Holy Spirit is the Environment of Transformation. If you ask for this baptism, I will never give you a serpent. I will answer you.

For the Holy Spirit is your Comforter, Counselor, Intercessor, Helper, Advisor. I have not left you Fatherless. You are not an orphan. To the widow, I have given Myself as Provision. I Am that Bread that satisfies. I Am the Kinsman-Redeemer. Come and possess your land. What has been stolen? What have the locusts eaten?

I have sold all to restore this to you.

Thrive in this environment. Receive the fleshy heart. Allow Me to renew a right spirit within you. Let Me do this transformational work. Rest, knowing that I Am even now re-making you in My image. In that Holy of Holies in your most secret chamber, your heart-house, I Am making newness of Life.

This is how you will know them. This is how you will know Me, and you will know yourself, the new creature you have become.

See the pearl within your fleshy heart. See that fruit within. Be the pearl. This is your true mission.

Day 19

A Day's Journey

Have you ever waited through the night for dawn to come? For the sun to give its first pale, pink light? For the birds to begin sing-songing their messages through the air? They announce the first light of day and have done so since the dawning of time.

For the adventurer, the first light of day announces the casting off, the launch. My favorite part of day was always this moment. First Light. Groaning against the light is a good indication of the futility of your days. Facing the day should not feel so empty as it sometimes has for you.

You realize, now, that this feeling of futility, of a prison-house of days lining up one like the other, is the fruit of works done to impress, works that strive to reach heaven, ever higher and greater works meant to get the attention of heaven. A proverbial Tower of Babel. But has heaven ever listened to the much-doing? The endless clamouring for accolades, the constant filling up of calendar dates in planners? The strategy sessions, the overbooked agenda? To look at this litany of events, one would think it constitutes a life.

But my sent ones went out with no provision, no planners, no agents, and no itinerary. My Good News is Manna for "Whosoever will." The laborer is worthy of his hire, I told them. I will give you what you should say in that hour. Not by might, not by power, but by My Spirit.

The anointing breaks the yoke, every yoke. One type of bondage is the illusion that one may work his or her way to God. The anointing is the rest, the lying down in green pastures. The Good Shepherd restores your soul. When you rise and see the first pale, pink light of day, you know the blank page that is before you, the unfilled planner, the unspent days waiting for you to grace them with adventure. You rise, a slayer of dragons, a person of enterprise, looking for possibilities.

Life in Me is an adventure. I Am the Chief Executive Officer of Surprise Appointments. A God of Uncharted Waters Am I. Have you ever been there before? No? Good. Go ye into all the world.

Be open to adventure. You will find, on your journey, places of respite along the way. Take a meal, a coffee, with someone you barely know. Let it be My Light that shines before men. Say, "Yes," to a God appointment. Help shoulder someone's load. Pray for them. Share your testimony. The people I send to you will listen. They are desperate. Despite all appearances, they have shown up today at this respite, at this God appointment, because I lead them to it. They have told me they are at the end of themselves. Go easy on them, love them back to Me. Lead them beside the still waters.

Chances are they knew Me, once, they were mine, but now they are like lost sheep scattered, beaten, and scared. Go ye and bring My sheep back into the fold.

Think back. Did not someone do this for you? Was there not someone ready to speak the right word at the right time and turn your thoughts back toward Me? Maybe your heart was hardened and someone showed, just for a moment, a little compassion, and your stony heart turned to flesh, and you felt stirrings, the awakening of the new creature. Maybe you were on the way to your adventure, to your becoming, and you got lost along the way. Maybe someone took the wind out of your sails, said or did something so grotesque, or maybe there was so great a loss, that you pulled down your sails, closed the hatches, and began endlessly drifting.

But the gifts of God are without repentance. My sheep know my voice. The shadow of death is an illusion only. I have defeated Death, and your pathway is alive with break of day. I Am the Breaker, the Breakthrough. I go before you to break barriers. I lead captivity captive, setting free those in bonds, healing the brokenhearted, bringing Good News, Good Tidings of Peace and Great Joy.

We are on this journey together. The Spirit of Grace has come, the hovering Hope of Your Days. I have not left you comfortless. I have given you this Counselor, an Advocate, a Helper, a Comforter. You are not alone. I will never leave you nor forsake you, even unto the end of this journey, to the end of your earthly life, to the end of the world. You do not have to carry such a heavy burden. Come and take My yoke, the anointing that shatters fetters, tethers, and the bonds that anchor your soul. My Holy Spirit is My Hope in you, My Grace toward you, My Faith bringing fruit, freedom, deliverance.

You are My Light, shining before men. When I look across the landscape, searching for My own, it is the lampstands, the beams of light keeping the darkness at bay, that I look for. I walk among those lampstands, those bright lights shining with My Truth. The Restrainer, as a force, holds back an onslaught of evil waiting just outside the doors. A Mighty Fortress is your God.

Every good and perfect gift cometh down from the Father of Lights. My Father has no fellowship with darkness. You were not meant to be tethered, anchored, weighed down with the cares of a world that is passing away.

Let the dead bury the dead.

You are meant for adventure. Steer your ship into the current. Face the oncoming storm, knowing the Holy One of Israel, the Mashiach Nagid, is on board your ship, and not one soul shall be lost! Take your ship into uncharted waters. Navigate the hard places.

Run toward Goliath with nothing but your five rocks and your confession. Let it be your vulnerability that brings My power to rest upon you. Fight the Good Fight of Faith. When Death, Sickness, Poverty, Fear, or Guilt come upon you, stand up to the giants and say, "Not today." Tell the giant in your life, "How dare you defame the name of the Holy One of Israel? Who comes out to defy the Lord My God?" Face your giant. Stare it down. Become a champion giant-killer.

I did not send these evil things into your life. I gave My Life for your abundance, so that you could live a large life, like My servant David, a man after my own heart. A lion. Let the devil take your measure and find My Power, My Love, a Sound Mind, the Mind of Yeshua Hamashiach, who defeated him and his angels. Let it be by Grace, that it might be by Faith. Triumph in My victory! Praise My name! Raise the banner of Love! March around your living room seven times and claim your land! Run the giants out of your inheritance! Rest, knowing I have conquered all and wait only for you to walk into your land and lay claim.

Take back your newborn birthright. Come, Prodigal, back to the Father. Wear the robe, the ring, the sandals. We'll kill the fatted calf, hold a festival, celebrate your homecoming. For the long season of summer is almost done in the House of the Lord, and the fields, they say to Me, "Harvest!" It is nearly time for the tables to be set. Come, and do not tarry, for the door is yet open but a moment.

Day 20

Castaway

The fact is, I always liked fishing. I mostly liked watching the actions of the fishermen. There are two ways to go: giant hauls in great nets, bringing up the manna of the sea, or, one at a time. This is by design.

The act of fishing one at a time mirrors the relationships of men with one another. There are lessons from the skills involved in fishing that echo My calling in your life. To gain abundance, substance, you must cast-away substance. You must risk something to gain much. The very act of casting is the initial step of deliverance.

Cast your care upon Him, for He cares for you.

I can't care for you if you aren't willing to cast all that you know far from you, into the deep. You must give me that tiny bit of sustenance you call a life. You must place it squarely on My shoulders, as the child gives his toy to his Father to be fixed, knowing His father will take the toy to His tool bench and make it new.

You are not the fixer. You have never truly fixed anything in your life. The more you tried, the worse it got. Am I not correct?

That tiny bit of bait is your life in your hands. You can keep the bait on the hook and never launch it.

Or you can cast it away.

Once you do this, control is illusion. This is what frightens you.

You still have the line tethered to the pole, but all that you have is put away from you. What fragility! It goes against everything you know. Anything could happen. A big fish could come up and steal your miniscule sustenance and leave you with nothing. You know this. You fear this. It could be Jonah and the Whale all over again. You could wind up in the belly of the whale, caught in the whale's snare, an irony that does not escape you.

You could catch a big fish, but it might take some skill to land the creature. You might have to navigate around some obstacles, stay the course, fight the good fight.

There is nothing you can give up that is worth missing My sustenance, My manna, nothing that is worth holding onto only to find you have missed Me. For your tiny bit of sustenance on the end of a fishing line, I will give you great store, great supply, endless sustenance. For a worm, I gave Peter a coin. It was in the fish's mouth. Do you not think, if he had continued baiting hooks and casting out, that every fish he pulled up would have had yet another coin? I do not give stones for bread, or serpents for fish.

When you put your sustenance far from you, it feels like it is everything. At that moment, you are measuring your life in coffee spoons, fragments of cloth, gas money, snack bars, milk money, tooth fairy deposits. This is not your life! This is bait: worms, crickets, the smelly fish-loving substances that bring them in. The harvest of seas awaits you! Cast away all that you hold dear. What have you considered sustenance that is truly bait to attract all the fruit of the sea? Are you hoarding your seed? Cast your old life, your earthly cares, far from you into the deep. That is where I Am. I fear not the billowing waves nor the depth of the deepest seas. That is where I live, where I do My best manna-festation.

Bring ye all the bait to the shore. Bait the hooks on lines. Line up the fishing poles and cast. You never know which line will bring in the big harvest! This is the adventure of possibility! Bring family, friends, to the seashore. Cast away care, the tiny bait you thought was your lot. Launch out into the deeper part of the river, waist high. Put your waders on and cast away.

Bring in the fish-harvest. Share your provision. Let's have a fire at the shore. I love a fish breakfast. That was the first meal I prepared with My hands for My disciples. Fish breakfast just after dawn. In My favorite time of day, we shared My own catch.

I love to watch children the first time they catch a fish. It is the joy of discovering the secret. How they love to cast the line. They have no fear. They have every expectation the fish will latch on to their bait.

Cast your little for a greater yield. Sacrifice that little to gain it all.

This is the secret of the kingdom. It is the Father's great pleasure to give it to you.

Day 21

A Day of Treasure

You have heard men say that trash and treasure are one and the same: the only difference, some say, is in the man himself. The Son of Man came to seek and to save that which is lost. Have you discovered what is treasure in your life and what is trash? Do ye have the wisdom to know one from another one? The tares and the wheat grow up together so as not to destroy or cast away all hastily.

For the Kingdom of God is as a Merchant seeking goodly Pearls. The Kingdom of Heaven is like a woman looking all over for her precious, lost coin. And when she finds it, she calls all her neighbors and friends over to rejoice with her.

What was once lost is now found.

Are you the keeper of the city dump, or are you a treasure-hunter?

He who keeps My Word, he who treasures My Word, in him, in her, the love of God has reached maturity. The fullness of the God-head resides in the hidden place of manna-festation. Arise, shine, for thy Light is come! Blindness to the deep things, the authentic gifts of God, is removed, and the Truth is made manifest for all to see! Build yourself up on your most holy faith. Rise up to the fullness of My stature. Keep the Treasure of My Word. Learn of Me. We have This Treasure in earthen vessels, hiding in plain sight.

The dragnet catches all without discernment or revelation. Governments seek to control all the people with laws that blanket and affect all the same, regardless of circumstance. Justice is blind, but My mercy endures forever. My tender mercies are new every morning. I Am that Fisher of Men, going after My children one at a time. The Law of that Spirit of Life in Yeshua Hamashiach has brought freedom from that old law of sin and death. You are truly free. You have a choice.

I have cast a line out to you, not a dragnet to bring you in by force. I know you, intimately. You hear My voice. Be still. Today, if you hear My voice, harden not your heart. Today is the day of salvation. I Am that Great Fisher of Men. Behold, I stand on the seashore, casting My Word out for a catch. He that hath an ear, let him hear. Faith cometh, do you not know this? I can do no more than to Provide Myself. Come unto Me, all ye that are heavy laden, and I will give you rest. Take My yoke upon you, for My yoke is easy, and My burden is light.

You fear that you will be put under bondage again, this time to religion, to a list of requirements, to subjection under the law. But the law and the prophets were until John the Baptist, to show the way to repentance and renewal. John, in the spirit of Elijah, said that he was not worthy to untie the shoes that I wore. The new dawn in the middle of the Jordan River, where Joshua created the twelve-stone monument, was the beginning of the Open Door. The Good News of the Gospel. There, for the price of repentance, they could come, one at a time, and receive My Word. My Word was Made unto Flesh, and My Word healed them.

The path to redemption is clear.

Have you ever witnessed a pure act of redemption? Redemption draweth nigh. It comes in many forms. The nurse on night shift telling jokes to the man who was just told the cancer was back. The mother giving the last chocolate cupcake to her two kids to split.

Your real life is hidden to protect it and to protect you.

Enter thou into this Joy. It is your strength. In this Joy, there is no sacrifice. We need no martyrs. There is nothing you can give up that is worth a hair on your head. Your value is priceless, your worth incalculable. I gave My Life for Adam. Would I do less for you? Adam was every man, Eve every woman. Now, I Am the Last Adam. Satan has no part in Me. I have redeemed you from the law of sin and death. They are cast away from you! Cast away with joy the strongholds, those things to which you cling that are of no value. I gave everything so you might have New Life in Me!

What great present can you give Me that would make up that sum? What religious doctrine? What self-sanctified works? Count the cost of casting away the dead things, those things that gratify flesh only, not just the physical body, but the very fabric of that old man who still wears the stench of death. That old creature wanders through dimly-lit streets, lost and calling out to the dead for company. The old man staggers under the weight of old addictions, lives in ash heaps in a burned down house.

Arise! Take up thy Life! Walk forth into Life Incarnate! Allow My Anointed One and His Anointing to break the yoke. What is restraining you, holding you back from your Promised Land? To what are you in bondage to the point that you no longer believe in freedom? From what do you need deliverance?

Do not delay.

Come up Hither. Find your flight path. Do you not know that planes fly at heights where there are no storms? Come up into the secret place. Hide yourself in the cleft of the Rock. Look down on the turmoil, the heat of battle, the strife. You have not been called to experience My wrath.

You are My beloved. Come up Hither.

Day 22

The Shaking

Beloved, I know you have noticed the shaking.

Some things are shifting, others are being shaken to their very foundations, to the core. The fabric of things is revealed in the peeling away of the veneer. The true nature of everything comes out eventually.

I know you sometimes feel that you are being shaken, but do not fear. I have not come to take spoil or to watch as some do, a guilty pleasure, the voyeurism of your age. I do not sit back and relish in your frustrations, your stumbling, your shame. For I see in secret and reward you in secret. My gifts never wax old.

This shaking, too, is transformation. For it is the final removal and upheaval of all that can be shaken so that which is permanent and unshakable can remain.

For who can fathom the firmament or chase the deepest underwater creatures to their homes? Who can counsel Leviathan to surface or to return to his hiding place?

Do not worry, Beloved. Not one hair of your head will perish.

For, I Am your Unshakable Core. I have given Myself, poured Myself into the vessel, that harbor prepared for My Habitation. The fathomless deep calls to deep.

Relationships are under scrutiny. Marriages are being tested. Storms are coming. Earthquakes are caused by friction, pressure built up as conflicting plates of earth shift and move across one another. People scream for tolerance but there is no tolerance, only conflicting agendas.

Beloved, there is movement, a shaking, in the heavenlies. In the atmosphere, where principalities and powers devise evil schemes; where the illusionist puts on a show for the masses, there is much shaking, much conflict, much friction. Spiritual forces are lining up for the last battle for the souls of the lost. Do ye not yet understand? The wheat grows up with the tares. The great imitator has placed wolves in sheep's clothing in the fellowship.

This shaking is a revelation, not a shaking intended for your suffering. You will find out who among you is standing on the Truth of My Word. You are the Redeemed. Let the Redeemed of the Lord say so. You are bought with a price. You will find out who loves the truth and who loveth and maketh a lie.

Love the Truth, Beloved. I Am the Way, the Truth, and the Life. The Truth is a firm foundation. Keep My Word as the foundation wherein you stand against the seduction of this present darkness. Beware of private doctrines, of seductive words, of emotional displays, of programs and much business. Beware of cult followings and large crowds and personalities.

Where there is conflict, there is likely to be growth. The seed breaks the ground, comes up from below the surface, breaks forth. Did I not tell you I Am the Breaker who goes before you? The Breakthrough.

Where My Word is preached, there may be division. For I have not come to bring harmony to the world, but to bring a sword for the dividing asunder of spirit and bone, flesh and the breath of life, manna and spoilage, truth and lies. The kingdom of God suffereth violence. Do not think that I have come to make peace with the world. I Am

Peace. My Peace I leave with you, but you must discern. There are many among you who will call you hostile for speaking the truth. Many will be offended. People can tolerate anything but the truth. Many will fall away from the faith; their love will grow cold. Their houses were built on sand. Since they love illusion, I will send them strong delusion, so they believe the lie of lies.

Seek Me while I may be found. The night is coming like a thief. If the house owner had known what time the thief was coming, he would have been prepared. If My people could see the moment I break through their defenses, their fortresses of self-seeking, their paper castles, they would be ready, but alas, they are not because they believe not.

Their lip service is far from Me.

Make ready. Prepare to receive. Get vessels and not a few. Fill every one. The night is coming when no man can work. Trim the lamps, keep them lit, for the shout is even now at the gates, "The Bridegroom cometh!"

Day 23

Forever

The Third Day.

A Marriage in Cana.

On the Third Day, God Created.

The Third Day, Twice, He called it "Good."

The Third Day is the Day of Double Blessing.

The Third Day, the Lord brought His Presence down from Mt. Sinai to be among His People.

Noah's Ark came to rest on the Third Day.

The Sabbath was made for man, but the Third Day was made for the Lord.

I Am the Lord who Blesses Thee.

The Son of Man rose on the Third Day. Three Days and Three Nights in the belly of the great fish.

This three-day period establishes the law of gestation. Cast your bread upon the water, for it shall return unto you after many days. How many? Do not count them. Does the woman with child waste the days counting? No. She prepares. Too much to do. She must get ready.

Do you feel as though you've waited forever? Have you said these very words? The pregnant woman waits through nine months, three sets of three, while her child, a seed, grows and occupies her belly and can no longer be contained. That child breaks forth, surfaces, swims up into life. The child grows into a man, a woman, develops, matures, passes into adulthood, middle age, old age, and finally unto death.

Harvest. Or is it?

Beloved, I Am the Resurrection and the Life. He that abideth in Me, though he were dead, yet shall he live.

You were not made for the harvest of death. You have already seen all of death you will ever see. Why do you yet fear it? Your flesh is as grass, as spindly plants cover the earth, as your clothes cover your body, and so, when this life is over, your flesh will fall away from you. It will be an act of reckless abandon, like tossing a worn-out set of clothes into the fire. You will look no more back on this covering, no more than you would look back on a tattered, threadbare shirt.

And yet, you will mourn, grieve the days you sacrificed for this heap of cloth, this waxing old garment, for which you often traded the things of eternity.

I have already given you Resurrection Life and My glory that covereth. I love to look upon a woman with long hair because her hair is her glory. I made woman this way to embody the glory: the seed within, the brilliant, long hair without, the life of sacrificial beauty. Her hair covers in brilliance and mystery. My glory covereth and yet shines, illuminated, made to command attention. In much the same way as a woman's hair can shine and move with freedom and mystery, the raiment I give you moves, shines, creates waves of brilliant color and light.

Even the beautiful Queen of Sheba marveled at the dancers in the temple, moving together in white raiment. You will dance, Beloved, in the streets of the Holy City, in your chambers, on the glassy sea. They will speak of our glory, our Communion, forever.

75

Your flesh is not forever. Why do you worry about that which, even now, is passing away? Even the Quantum Physicists say that this dimension is a simulation. How do you know the nature of your reality? When you look in the mirror, are you really seeing the self? Or is the self even real? Did you make the self up in an attempt to put the best spin on your life? The corporal narrative, as it were?

Do you not know that I Am the Lover of your soul? I know you intimately. Your real life is hid with Me, a secret life no one knows. The flesh craves attention, wants fame, the easy way. The Pharisees ring bells, command attention, wait for an audience, when they give to the poor. They take pictures and post them on social media for all to see. They have their reward. Your secret life is in seed form only. You can live to be 120 and never arrive. You are Forever my child. What more do you need? To whom are you looking for approval? To the world?

The world is already dead.

Your life in secret is lived in quiet places where we meet. We Abide Forever. Communion Forever. If a man love me, he will keep my words: and my Father will love him, and we will come unto him, and make our abode with him. I never left you, not for a minute. You can't run far enough. I Am Already There.

Before you conceived of running away, I Am.

Jonah ran away from Me. Even in disobedience, he found me. I told him to go east. He went west and found Me already in the cabin of the ship, in Joppa, circumventing the earth three score, passing him countless times and walking on the water off the shores of Tarshish, waiting for the Big Fish to swallow him up.

I have told you before of my love of fishing.

The irony. Big Fish catches Man.

The original Big Fish story, but not the way you usually hear it.

Even in Sheol, the Son of Man was not out of My Father's Reach.

After suffering for the sins of all men, YHVH spoke in the midst of My Spirit, "Thy throne, Oh God, is Forever!" The Father proclaimed the Son of Man as the Conquering YHVH. We are Three in One.

There's that number again.

On the Third Day, the powers of hell were the first witnesses to The Resurrection. For if Satan himself had known My Resurrection Power, he would never have crucified the Lord of Glory. Death was swallowed up. It hath no more power over you.

Of what are you so afraid? Dying? Take off your coat, your shirt. That incarnation of you is now dead.

Get the picture?

Your flesh fears pain, recoils from want, but you were made for Life Abundant, to Abide with Me, forever. Be ye transformed from the fleeting desires of your flesh. What are you protecting yourself from? Do you not yet know how much I Love you? Can you not fathom the depth of Love that breaks, the seed come to maturity, breaking forth through the earth, to stand, in full power, the first-fruits? The first-born from the dead?

I Am the Breaker, the quintessential Break-Through!

Do you not know that you have already taken part in My Resurrection?

Except a corn of wheat fall into the ground and die, it abideth alone: but if it die, it bringeth forth much fruit.

I have done all the dying you will ever do.

We shall not all sleep, but we shall all be changed.

I Am the Resurrection and the Life. This Life I give you, now, to live in Me. The Spirit of Life in Me has made you free from the law of sin and death.

Be ye transformed.

Throw off the shackles you wear, the pain that paralyzes. Throw away dead doctrine. Cast the idols into the trash, the false gods for which you all but sacrifice each minute of your life.

Take out the trash. Cast mountains into seas.

Cast out into the deep. Launch into your life.

Let the dead bury the dead.

Forever has already started.

Come up, Hither.

Day 24

A Day of Loaves and Fishes

So many statements in the Gospels begin, "I Am . . .You are."

Vine. Branches

Light. Lampstands.

Word. Salt.

On the shores of Galilee, loaves of bread and fishes from the sea came together to feed the multitude. Many teach this to illustrate faith as a creative force, and that is true. The substance was multiplied in My hands, and the disciples fed all the multitude with plenty left over.

Seven baskets full.

Seven is the number of completion, wholeness, perfection, and maturity. Six symbolizes man without God.

The simple child's lesson here is in the bread and fishes; God and redeemed man must come together to feed, or rather, provide all, everything, complete sustenance, for the multitude.

I Am the God of the Fish Lunch. That you may know that I Am the Great Fisher of Men, I used a child's meal, the smallest provision, to provide, exponentially, for all.

I look for simple obedience. Catching men, one at a time, with a simple child's meal. Give them sustenance, bring them out of the highways and hedges, invite the poor to your table.

For I have given you a table and sustenance enough to share. I Am the Lord of exponents, the God of Increase, the Expert in algorithms, vectors, calculus, and hyperspaces. I operate outside of space-time. You have no way to fathom the length, breadth, width, height, the multiple dimensions of my yield. Does a crop not come from tiny seeds? Have you not seen fields covered with wildflowers?

What is your part?

Place your sustenance into My Hands.

I assure you, I can be trusted. He that lendeth to the poor lendeth to Me, and I will repay.

I'm good for it.

Give, and it shall be given unto you, good measure, pressed down, shaken together and running over shall men give unto your bosom.

Did the child lack for anything?

To whom was given the seven baskets leftover?

The Gospel does not record this.

You must know, from studying My Word, that the child who supplied the fish lunch took seven baskets home. His family had to help him carry the increase. They had enough to call their friends for a meal and to give thanks before their friends who became witnesses of My Father's goodness.

I know My plans for you, plans to prosper you.

Put away ideas of stardom, of "arrival," at some place where the masses applaud your work.

How many of My people were ever applauded? Was I? Does the world applaud Me now? No, rather, the world mocks Me.

Gratitude is a profitable response, but approval is dangerous. Beware of those who receive the approval of many. The stamp and seal of men means nothing to Me. I have nothing in the world's celebrities. Most are substance abusers; some live their lives in total darkness. The light of the stage and screen is the only light they know. They know, above all others, that they are not worthy of the worship they receive. Their sin is the sin of the former cherub, the fallen angel. They have taken their reward already. There is nothing more.

This fish story is one of humility. A child's meal. Simple Obedience. The Good News. The Communion of God and Men. The Blessing of the Lord. Increase.

Ye are more than conquerors through Me. Your life is not a destination. You understand so little of the nature of eternity. It is not linear. It is not chronological. You will never arrive because you are already Here.

In My Hands.

I Am the Bread of Life.

Share Your Bread. Go out and be ye fishers of men. Rest in the Eternity of My Ultimate Provision.

Day 25

A Day of Forgiveness

Beloved: Do you know you have spiritual eyes? With these gifts of perception I have instilled within you, you can discern, see the thoughts and intents of the heart, see the potential in people. Yes, you can also see the hurt in others. Did ye not know that woundedness is an identifier? My sheep need tending. They have been wounded by ravenous wolves in sheep's clothing whose self-interest was paramount, whose god was themselves. Marriages, friendships, family relationships, fellowships, so many ships wrecked on the rocks, each member attempting to captain his fate, each pulling his own way.

Run to me; jump out of the boat. Be not afraid of the power of My Holy Spirit, that Comforter who waits for you to run to Him. He has ushered in blessing, all spiritual blessing in heavenly places. Have I not told you? I have come that you might have Life in its fullest manifestation. The fish are jumping! Your bounty awaits! Why would you stay in that ghost-ship one minute longer?

Have you not heard it? We are building a habitation, a tabernacle for My Holy Spirit, saith the Lord, made without hands, whose builder and maker is God, with Living Stones to harbor My restraining power on earth. You will see lives changed. Do not look only for miracles, but look instead for changed lives by My Hand, saith the Lord. Children coming back to their parents like lost sheep returning to the sheepfold. Young people turning to Me, knowing Me like no other generation before. Young Davids and Deborahs coming forward to trust Me with all they have. Restoration.

That is My work, and I Am about it in this time, saith the Lord. I Am that Chief Cornerstone, and I Am well able to satisfy My Body with Life Abundant, the Blessing of Abraham which has come on the gentiles through faith, a new and better covenant. Let it be by Grace, saith the Lord. If any man or woman, boy or girl, is thirsty, let him or her come to Me, and I will give the water of life freely and without price.

My healing power works in enclaves of spiritual resonance where the harmony of My communion rings out as My people praise Me. I inhabit that praise. Even the rocks would cry out if My people didn't lift up their voices in praise. It doesn't have to be perfectly accompanied worship music penned by career songwriters. I desire My children's praises as any parent does. I love to hear My children lift up their voices. In out of the way places, coffee houses, parking lots, grocery stores, My name is whispered in the very streets. Can you hear it?

Everywhere you go, people are speaking My name and recounting the Blessings in their lives. The joy of the Lord brings strength to feeble knees and bent backs, straightens the limbs for the mission, makes straight paths for your feet. Find My people and go to them. I will give you sustenance to share and the words to say. Be not afraid, for My presence has gone before you. I Am the Breaker of strongholds, the Shoulder you can cry on, the Banner of Love raised high and lifted up over you.

Cast out the root of bitterness, the eye that sees all through the pain of past wounds. Cast out the root of unforgiveness. Stop giving your power away to others. Hate and anger are the weakest emotions. Only someone you truly love and care about could make you that angry. Are you going to tell me that a mere acquaintance, someone at work, someone on the highway, a family member you rarely see, has this much power over you? To the pure, all things are pure. Whatsoever things are lovely, whatsoever things are of a good report, whatsoever things are true, think on these things. Are you ready to give up the bitterness that colors your whole world, a root you have never torn up out of your ground, the resentment, the sense of failure? Are you ready to stand on the Rock that is My Name?

Can you put away dead things? If your right eye offend thee, pluck it out.

I Am the Chief Cornerstone. Do you not understand that you are a living stone, your body a temple containing My consuming fire? Flesh and blood cannot inherit the kingdom of God. Are you in lack, want, deep need? My fire consumes all that is not of Me. Do you dare to tell your brother he must cast out the splinter in his eye when you tolerate a beam that would support an entire house in yours? Cast down imaginations and every high thing constructed, a fortress standing between you and the world, between you and Me. Do you not yet understand the kingdom of God is within you?

Tear down these fortresses the flesh builds to separate you from My Love. Tear down these strongholds of indignation and resentment!

Your foundation must be built on the Rock that is higher than anything you can ask or think. I Am Love Incarnate. My Love cannot be shaken. I cannot have fellowship with hate. Fear not what men can do unto you. Fear the One who can put both soul and body in Gehenna. Hate isolates, casts you away from Me, eternally. Do not rationalize your anger. Don't let the sun go down upon your wrath. There is no earthly or heavenly reason for you to be so angry.

Vengeance is Mine, saith the Lord. The person who has so much control over you is Mine. Pray for your enemies. To be angry is easy. Pray for those who despitefully use you, persecute you, for so did they persecute the prophets before you.

So did they persecute Me.

Have you been mocked? So have I.

Have you been abused? So have I.

Have you lost? I have, too.

Did you do anything to be born?

No, of course not. So it is with the second birth. This righteousness created in you, your transformed being, is not of your work. You have not accomplished this, not even in the act of coming to Me, for I have called you.

You have not rescued yourself. You are born again, not of corruptible seed but of incorruptible. Do you know what this means? Incorruptible means nothing, no one, can soil, destroy, break down, harm, hurt, break, bend, corrode, corrupt, or kill it.

Don't take your own measure by comparing yourself to others. "Well at least I don't. . . ." Such is foolishness. Pride says you were instrumental in your own deliverance. Pride says your Lord's arm was shortened to save and you had to get in the act.

Let it never be thought.

Humble yourself under the mighty hand of God, and He will exalt you in due time.

Root up the cause of bitterness, which is pride in self. Your pride was hurt. Someone threatened your "self." Consider yourself stricken, smitten along with Me. Let the old man die, let her be crucified with Me. Rise up, receive the power of My Resurrection Life. Get up from the bed of affliction. Rise up, that new creature. Be ye transformed. Receive your new name. Ride alongside Me on your white horse. You will one day judge angels. Do you not know this?

But it will not be in the fragility of your ego that you will judge. It will be in the Light of My Truth, the Word of the Living God. Learn it well.

For I long to write My Law into your hearts.

This is a very personal work. Only My hands are to touch your heart, Beloved.

Let not another write upon your heart.

I Am a jealous Lord.

Day 26

A Day of Release

You have been grieving, My Love. Yes, forgiveness doesn't always mean the bond will remain. Human bonds are fragile, are they not? Beloved, not every person who comes into your life is permanent. Have I not told you? The wind bloweth where it listeth, and thou hearest the sound thereof, but canst not tell whence it cometh, and whither it goeth: so is every one that is born of the Spirit.

I know what is in man's heart. You have bound yourself to people who are not yoked together with you in such a commitment. You have often found that you are doing all the committing and that others benefit but have not partnered together with you in commitment.

This is what I meant when I said you can't always tell where a wind has come from and where it will go. This is why I did not commit to some in Jerusalem who saw My miracles and believed in Me. They believed in what I could do, but they did not believe in who I Am.

Therefore, they could not take up their cross and follow Me all the way to the garden of Gethsemane, to the darkest hour. If a person to whom you have committed cannot follow you through your darkest hour, this reveals who they truly are. They are with you for your gifts and not for You.

Do not be afraid, Beloved. I, too, have been on the receiving end of such rejection, such bold-faced selfishness. Are you surprised? Many seek Me for what I can give them. They ask Me for things, but they have no desire to know Me. This is what I will have to acknowledge in the Last Days. "Depart from Me, for I never knew you."

Those who saw My miracles sought Me for the miracles. In these days of apostasy, many call upon Me. They cry, "Lord, Lord." Like the Pharisees, they seek Me for their own selfish ends. What I will not do is commit to them.

This communion, this union, is Everything you are and Everything I Am, eternally. This is the ultimate marriage, although there has never been a marriage that meets this level of commitment. I Am with you always, even unto the ends of the earth. Love is stronger than death, Beloved. Stronger than Sheol. You will never face Gehenna, nor suffer isolation from Me. There is no place you can go that I Am not, My Love.

Nothing and no one can separate you from the Lover of your soul. I Am that Lover.

Do not fret that this person has not lived up to his commitment or that person isn't a true friend as you had thought. The wind is blowing mightily, My Love, shaking foundations. Those who will fall away will do so without affecting the commitment I have for you and that you have for Me. Our union is unshakable. This house is unbreakable. This tabernacle of Love is our forever home.

Release yourself from bondage to the uncommitted.

Take back your land! Take back your heart! Do not allow unbelievers, scoffers, and the hangers-on, the burden-bringers, to stay. Put them on their way. The wind blew them in.

Let it blow them back out again.

Not by might, not by power, but by my Spirit.

Perhaps they were in your life for a time. Perhaps that season is over. The winds are changing.

Release yourself and let go of that old season. Embrace the sweet smell of harvest-time. Let the wind blow the dead things out of your life. The vultures only gather around dead bodies, love.

That is not you.

The new wine is better, Love.

Arise.

Come up, hither.

Day 27

A Day Stripped Bare

Now that we have moved past the root of it to the losses you have experienced, those things that have fallen away from you, upon which you depended so, we are getting to the core of your fear.

No, it is not the enemy that is storming your gates. I Am the Door. The gates of hell shall never prevail against you, Love. You have freedom in Me to come in, go out, and find sustenance. I Am that Bread of Life, your Manna. I Am your Shelter

But your fear is that you will lose everything.

You fear that you will be stripped to the bone, your home, your livelihood, your freedom.

It doesn't take much to instill such a fearful prospect, does it My Love?

But I have not paid such an unparalleled purchase price for so great a pearl, for My miracle fruit of the sea, to leave you in the sands of time, undiscovered, lost, and alone.

I own the cattle on a thousand hills.

They are yours.

Mine are the fishes and all the life of the seas.

I Am the husbandman, the vinedresser, the vineyard owner. The heavens and the cosmos belongs to the Lord but the Earth has He given to the children of Men.

To you, I have committed My precious Son. You have been raised up together in Him, granted all spiritual blessings in heavenly places in Christ Jesus. You are joint-heirs with My Son. Do ye not know this?

In Him, you live, and move, and have your being. You are My child!

That is your freedom. I have ordained it. In My grace, you can come and go and live, freely.

Do not fear, Beloved.

You thirst and hunger for Me. I dwell with you. We abide together. We take our meals together, drive to work together, take our coffee, together. I inhabit the praises of My people. Eye hath not seen, nor ear heard, what has been prepared for you from the foundation of the world for those who love Me.

I know that you never wanted this. You never planned to break right down the middle. You didn't know that your bond was not permanent.

But, Beloved, I did.

I Am not afraid of men or women. Their ignorant words, their actions, do not define you, nor do they instill apprehension in Me.

This experience did not catch Me unprepared, My child.

Draw around your place of prayer a chalk-line that looks like Me. Draw hard lines as boundaries. Draw the chalk-line in your mind larger and larger until you and I exist in a space the size of the universe.

You determine who gets to be in a room with you. No matter what that person has done to you, they cannot have any space to inhabit. Do not give them that power. Yes, I know. Some violations are so personal, the wound so deep. Yes, I know this. I feel this pain already. That is why I bore those wounds, those gaping holes in my wrists, those deep chasms formed repeatedly by whips and Roman torture devices. Those stripes, those thorns, I bore all of that and more. Your pain was the reason. I came to bind up the brokenhearted. Isn't that you? You may as well give that, even that, the unspeakable pain, to Me.

But do not allow anyone to stay in your spiritual room if you don't want them there. Do not let them have your heart. Your heart is Mine and Mine alone.

All your borders are peace.

All your borders are safety.

Great is your peace and undisturbed composure.

Even if all is taken from you, you and I together will walk into a New Dawn with the power to create a better life than you have ever known.

That is My Resurrection Power operating in you.

Do I sense Hope? That is the first fruit of Resurrection. That is the Hope of this Gospel to which I've called you.

Dare to Hope, Beloved.

Behold, I Am coming soon.

Good News, My Love!

And My reward is with Me.

Day 28

A Day of Proclamations!

Behold, the Lamb of God, who taketh away the sins of the world! Who has declared all things from of old? Have not I, the Lord? There is no other God besides me! There is none besides Me.

Look to Me and be saved, all the ends of the earth! For I Am Lord, YHVH, and there is no other. I have sworn by Myself, the word is gone out of My mouth in righteousness and shall not return unto Me void. Every knee shall bow, every tongue shall swear that I Am the Lord. They will look upon Me whom they have pierced, and they will weep.

Only in the Lord shall one say, "I have righteousness and strength."

Even to your old age I am He and even to hair white with age will I carry you. I have made, and I will bear; yes, I will carry and will save. To whom will you liken Me and make Me equal and compare Me that we may be alike?

I declare the end from the beginning and from ancient times the things that are not yet done, saying, My counsel shall stand, and I will do all My pleasure and purpose. I have spoken, and I will bring it to pass; I have purposed it, and I will do it.

You have heard these things foretold; now you see this fulfillment; and will you not bear witness to it? I show you new things from this time forth, hidden things kept in reserve, which you have not known. They are created now, called into being by the prophetic word and not long ago, before today, you never heard of them, lest you should say, Behold, I knew this!

Yes, My hand has laid the foundation of the earth, and My right hand has spread out the heavens; when I call to them, they stand forth together to do My will.

Come near to Me and listen. The Lord your God caused the waters to flow forth from the Rock. My hand is not shortened but mighty to save.

I, the Lord, have declared your end from your beginning. I lead you beside the springs, beside the still waters. I know how to restore your soul. I bring you into green pastures.

Humble yourself. My hand is mighty. I Am the Resurrection and the Life. Enter in through the narrow gate; find the path less traveled to the straight gate. You have heard this word. Remnant. Let me exalt you, lift you above all that you know how to do.

Has your effort gotten you anywhere?

Release yourself from the prison of your soul. The prison of guilt. The prison of never-enough, of righting wrongs, of solving problems. Are things any better for your efforts?

Come to Me, all ye who are heavy laden. Take My yoke, for My burden is easy

The invoice is light, and I have already paid it in full.

Come up hither.

Day 29

A Day to Rise Up

With a thundering, a shaking, a trembling, and a rattling, the bones in the dry valley came together, rose up, and flesh came over them. From the four winds, the spirit brought spirit and breath upon these flesh-covered bones, and they rose up!

So it will be at the end of the age. The dead in Christ shall rise first. Then those who are alive and remain will be caught up together in the air.

So shall ye ever be with Me.

Do not fear for those who have gone on before. I can call up sons of Abraham from the stones in the road. Do you not think I can breathe new life into your loved ones?

What else in your life needs My breath, the Spirit of Life in Me?

What else needs Resurrection?

Beloved, this Breath of Life in Me knows no bounds. Love is stronger than death, Beloved, stronger than Sheol. My fragrance is from ointments poured out, My Life given for you, raising you up in power, to Life Everlasting. Beloved, we have an Everlasting Covenant made between YHVH and Me, Yeshua Hamashiach, Jesus the Anointed One. I came out from the Father, out from the Light-Energy of YHVH, a man in the God-head! I hold you in the palm of My hand. You in Me, I in the Father. This is our communion, and you cannot slip away.

Our Hands hold you.

To the end of the age and beyond, you are Mine by the unbroken covenant sealed in My blood.

I know the meaning of the word "commitment."

I will never leave you nor forsake you.

I've got you. Now, and for all time.

You are Mine.

Day 30

A Declaration of Love

Your Maker is your Husband.

Do I not know you better than anyone? Who else is there who truly knows you?

You have lived as a widow, wooed in youth and now scorned, forsaken.

But I have not forsaken you.

With great compassion and tender mercies, I gather you to Myself. My Bride once knew reproach, but now, she breaks forth in white raiment like the morning.

Many waters cannot quench love, neither can floods drown it. If a man would offer all the goods of his house for love, he would be utterly scorned and despised.

I have given all in love for your love, to have your love, to redeem you unto Myself in Love.

Though the mountains depart and the hills be shaken, yet My love and kindness shall not depart from you, nor shall My covenant of peace be removed.

Nothing broken, nothing missing, nothing damaged, nothing lost.

It is a Covenant of Completeness, My Beloved.

Come, ye afflicted, storm-tossed and not comforted. Do you not know that I have set your stones of fair colors, your white raiment a glorious reflection of Me? Your Bridegroom calls. Have you put on My Righteousness, the garment I have provided for you?

Behold, I come, My voice is heard in the streets. It is not much longer, and I will not tarry, I come suddenly, at such a time when there is heard a mockery, the ridicule of other women, the unfaithful among you. They will say you wait for nothing, that I Am not coming. "Where is your Beloved gone?" they will ask. "Where is He hiding himself? For we would seek him."

But, behold, I Am even at the doors. He who now restraineth the evil one will soon be lifted up out of the way. Like John, you will hear the great voice of many waters say, "Come."

The Spirit and the Bride say, "Come."

In My Father's House are mansions enough. I Am gathering you under My wings.

Come, My Beloved. Rise up on My wings of Love, borne on the winds of My Spirit, My Resurrection Life. Rise up on wings as eagles.

There is a dawn of Hope ahead, like no other, and yet, like every other. Like those first, pink rays of dawn say, "Adventure! Set sail!"

Fly! Make haste! Enter thou into the Joy of the Lord!

Come up Hither."

About the Author

After tying with Jars of Clay for the Song of the Year Contest at the Dove Awards, Andrea Mosier completed a BA in English. Her short story, "Mass" was a finalist for the Eric Hoffer Award for Prose in 2014, and her novel, *Fire Eater*, shortlisted for the Dundee International Book Awards in 2015. "The Illuminated Man" appeared in *Serendipity's* inaugural edition. After a two-year battle with Lyme Disease, Andrea was miraculously healed through intensive intercessory and hands-on prayer in addition to a revolution in food choices and lifestyle. Besides teaching creative writing to at-risk kids, Andrea helps homeless women with children through a rental assistance program called Manna Place.